BIRDS OF THE PACIFIC NORTHWEST MOUNTAINS

The Cascade Range, the Olympic Mountains,
Vancouver Island, and the Coast Mountains

JAN L. WASSINK

Mountain Press Publishing Company
Missoula, Montana
1995

Fifth Printing, June 2004

Cover photos copyright © 1995 Jan L. Wassink
Front cover: Mountain Bluebird
Back cover: Pine Grosbeak

Library of Congress Cataloging-in-Publication Data

Wassink, Jan L.
    Birds of the Pacific Northwest mountains :   the Cascade Range, the
Olympic Mountains, Vancouver Island, and the Coast Mountains /   Jan
L. Wassink.
      p.   cm.
    Includes bibliographical references and index.
    ISBN 0-87842-308-7 : $14.00
    1. Birds—Northwest, Pacific. 2. Birds—Northwest, Pacific—
Identification. 3. Mountain fauna—Northwest, Pacific. I. Title.
QL683.N75W37   1995   94-36360
598.29795—dc20   CIP

Printed in Hong Kong by Mantec Production Company

Mountain Press Publishing Company
P.O. Box 2399 • Missoula, MT 59806
406-728-1900

Dedicated to my mother,
Kathryn Wassink,
whose quiet encouragement
will never be forgotten.

Contents

Pacific Northwest Mountain System

This book covers the region including the mountain ranges that parallel the Pacific Coast and extend from Lassen Peak in northern California northward to the Bella Coola River in central British Columbia.

The Cascade Mountains, a range of heavily timbered, rugged volcanic mountains that stretch nearly 700 miles from southern British Columbia to the north end of the Sierra Nevada Range in northern California, are the dominant mountains in the region. East of the Cascades lie the Columbia Plateau of Washington and northern Oregon and the desert country of the Great Basin in southern Oregon and northern California. To the west lie the deep, fertile valleys that separate the Cascades from the coastal mountains of Washington, Oregon, and California.

The Olympic Mountains cover most of the Olympic Peninsula of Washington. The Strait of Juan de Fuca, which separates the Olympics from the Vancouver Island Ranges on the north, and Hood Canal, which separates the Olympics from the Cascades on the east, form ineffective barriers to flying birds. Consequently, the species found here are virtually identical to those of the Cascades, although they may be found in different proportions due to climatic and vegetative differences.

Likewise, the Inland Passage, which separates the Insular Range (represented in this book by the mountains of Vancouver Island and Queen Charlotte Island) from the Coast Mountains of British Columbia, does not limit the free movement of birds. The limits of distribution are climatic and vegetative.

Beginning at the Fraser River, just north of the Canadian–United States border and extending north to the Bella Coola River, lie the Coast Mountains of British Columbia. While the Cascades are largely volcanic in the south and grade into metamorphic rock interspersed with granite in the north, the Coast Mountains are mostly granite interspersed with remnants of metamorphic rock.

Climatic differences across the region are often extreme. From west to east across the region, the mountains themselves cause the climatic variation. The high mountain peaks force upward large, moist air masses moving easterly off the Pacific Ocean, causing the clouds to cool and release much of their water content on the western slopes of the ranges. Relieved of their moisture as they cross the crests of the Cascade and Coast ranges, those air masses have little precipitation to drop on the parched lands to the east. This rain shadow causes vastly different plants to grow on the west and east slopes.

In contrast, the differences in climate and vegetation from north to south are largely caused by latitude. The southern Cascades are the warmest and driest mountains in the region; the northern reaches of the Coast Mountains are cool, wet, and dotted with ice fields.

These climatic and vegetative gradients result in a rich and diverse array of bird life in the region. Birders seeking to sample this diversity may roam habitats from marshy shores, sagebrush flats, and agricultural cropland on the valley floors to expansive montane forests at the mid-elevations and alpine meadows and ice-covered mountaintops that exceed 14,000 feet. Numerous wildlife refuges—including Pitt-Addington Wildlife Management Area and Serpentine Wildlife Area in British Columbia, Nisqually National Wildlife Refuge (NWR) and Ridgefield NWR in Washington, Baskett Slough NWR and Klamath Basin NWR in Oregon, and Tule Lake NWR in California—protect important habitat for migrating and nesting waterfowl. Wilderness areas, national monuments, national recreation areas, and national parks cover parts of the area and maintain some of the beauty and integrity of the region's wildlife habitats. The Canadian Ministry of Environment and the United States Forest Service and the Bureau of Land Management manage other wide expanses for multiple use, one of which is wildlife values. The Pacific Mountain System provides excellent opportunities for careful observers to enjoy the bounty of bird life.

Introduction

Approximately 30 million people across North America are fascinated by birds, and more become interested every day. This book provides beginning bird-watchers with an easy-to-use field guide to some common and distinctive birds of the Cascades.

When I became interested in birds, more than 20 years ago, just seeing a brightly colored bird was excitement enough. Soon I wasn't satisfied until I knew its name. Even being able to identify the birds didn't satisfy my curiosity for long, and my questions soon went beyond "What is it's name?" to "What does it eat?", "Where does it go in the winter?", "Where does it nest?", "Why do I only see it in shallow water?", and so on. This book provides answers to many questions you will ask as your interest in birds deepens and your knowledge expands.

How to Use This Book

The Birds of British Columbia (vols. I and II), the checklists of North Cascades National Park, Mount Rainier National Park, Crater Lake National Park, Olympic National Park, and the twelve national wildlife refuges in Washington, Oregon, and northern California indicate that of the 800 or so species of birds seen in North America, almost 350 species have been observed in the Pacific Northwest mountains.

I chose most of the 197 species included in this book on the basis of ease of identification and the likelihood that a beginning birder will observe them. I also included a few species that are particularly colorful, particularly rare, or that have unusual behavior patterns. Whenever possible, I chose at least one species to represent each of the families of birds found in this region.

The nomenclature of this book follows the *Checklist of North American Birds*, sixth edition, published by the American Ornithologists' Union. To identify a bird, simply locate its photo in the book and glance across the page to learn its name. You will see two names there: a Latin name and a common name. The common name is probably the one you will learn first, but the Latin name will help you recognize relationships between different species.

Scientists classify birds, like all living organisms, according to their physical similarities and differences. The seven divisions in this classification system are—from most general to most specific—kingdom, phylum, class, order, family, genus, and species. A species includes individuals that exhibit virtually identical characteristics and breed with each other when given the opportunity. A genus consists of one or more similar species that do not interbreed. The names of these two groups, the genus and the species, make up the Latin name. In this classification system, each species has a unique scientific name. A scientist in France, reading about *Turdus migratorius,* knows that he is reading about the American robin rather than the one found in Europe, which is a different species.

To avoid looking at every photo each time you wish to identify a new bird, study the general characteristics (size, shape, behavior, and habitat) in the family introductions, skim through species descriptions, and study the photos. When you can recognize an unfamiliar water bird as a grebe, you can go directly to the grebe photos for species identification without wasting time looking through the duck section as well.

Ferruginous Hawk
J. L. WASSINK

Red-winged Blackbird displaying   J. L. WASSINK

If you spend much time birding, you will eventually see a bird that you cannot match with a photo in this book. Some species are dimorphic, meaning the sexes have different color patterns. If only the male is pictured here, you can often identify females of that species, particularly during the breeding season, by the company they keep. For example, if a male bufflehead is swimming alongside a small brownish duck of approximately the same size and shape, check the written description of the female bufflehead. If that doesn't match, you may be viewing a species that is not included here. In other cases, particularly the buteo hawks, the species may have different color phases within the species. The snow goose, for instance, has a white and a "blue" phase, and many hawks exhibit more than one color phase. For illustrations of species and color phases that this book does not cover, you will need to consult a more comprehensive field guide (see Suggested References).

The **Field Marks** describe characteristics of the bird that you will probably be able to see in the field. The size, an important factor in identifying birds, leads the list. The measurements, given in inches, indicate the length from the tip of the bill to the tip of the tail as seen in the wild. The measurements define an average length for that species; individuals may be larger or smaller. At first, you may have trouble differentiating between a 5-inch and a 6-inch bird, but as you gain experience and develop a feel for the size of familiar species, you will begin to recognize that a new bird looks slightly larger or smaller than a familiar species.

While many species may resemble each other superficially, each species has a specific combination of characteristics that identify it. I have highlighted those identifying characteristics with bold type. The rest of the field marks section outlines general features of the bird. The "parts of a bird" illustrations at the end of the book identify the terms used in this section.

Because the written word cannot do justice to bird songs and calls, I have included them only where they are particularly distinctive and/or necessary for identification. If you are interested in learning to bird by ear as well as by sight, consider purchasing one or more of the tape sets listed in the Suggested References at the end of the book.

The **Status** relates the general areas of the region the bird occupies, the abundance in those areas, the seasons to look for it there, and the bird's breeding status in the region. I have abbreviated the names British Columbia (BC), Vancouver Island (VI), North Cascades National Park (NCNP), Olympic National Park (ONP), Mount Rainier National Park (MRNP), and Crater Lake National Park (CLNP).

Definitions of abundance are subjective at best, but the following terms will prove helpful:

- An abundant bird is one that you are likely to see 25 or more of per day when looking in the appropriate habitat during the appropriate season.
- A common bird is one you probably will see daily when looking in the right habitat during the right season.
- Fairly common birds are likely to be seen once every 3 days.
- Uncommon birds will be seen probably only once in a week of looking.
- Rare birds appear only a few times each year.
- Irregular species are abundant at times but extremely rare most of the time.

The above terminology addresses only the numbers of a species present in the region. The following terminology describes when you will most likely to see a particular bird in this region and whether it breeds while it is here:

- A resident bird lives in the region year-round.
- A summer resident is present only in spring and summer.
- A breeder nests and raises young within the region.
- Winter visitors frequent the region between mid-December and late February.
- Migrants travel through the area on their annual spring or fall migrations.
- Vagrants do not normally visit the region but may occasionally wander through.

Observing Birds

There really is no "best place" to watch birds. Many people travel to national parks or wildlife refuges to view birds. If you are looking for a particular species that inhabits or is particularly abundant in only one area, that may be the best place to go. Birding can also fit easily into your daily activities. I do much of my birding while I am doing other things. I watch from my living room while I am relaxing or keeping one eye on a football game. I often bird in my backyard while feeding my llamas or doing yard work. I also bird from my vehicle while traveling to or from work or other appointments.

When I devote time exclusively to birding, I need not venture farther afield than my backyard—5 acres of Douglas fir, a reclaimed apple orchard, and numerous thickets and weed patches. Home to a wide variety of species, it is also readily accessible—I can sneak in a few minutes of birding before and after work or perhaps while I should be mowing the lawn. By finding a good place to bird close to home, you can familiarize with yourself with an area and the birds that frequent it. You can discover where their territories are, where they feed, where they nest, and how they behave.

Still, birding in new territory, looking for new species and watching huge concentrations of birds in staging areas or on breeding grounds is too exciting to overlook. To locate worthwhile sites, talk to local birders or check with your state wildlife officials and the wildlife refuges in the region. For example, large concentrations of wintering bald eagles can be viewed in Harrison River/Kilby

A young bird-watcher gets a close look at a nighthawk.   J. L. WASSINK

Provincial Park in British Columbia and in the Klamath Basin National Wildlife Refuges—Upper Klamath NWR in Oregon and Lower Klamath NWR and Tule Lake NWR in California. The eagles begin arriving in November, with the number of these beautiful birds peaking at over 500 in January and February. They depart in late March or early April. An area near you may have similar concentrations of birds.

The best time to watch birds is anytime you can. Your viewing success and enjoyment will increase greatly if you look for particular birds when they are most active. Common nighthawks are most active at dusk, when they begin patrolling in search of flying insects. Likewise, owls are most active at night, and hummingbirds, during the day

You can bird effectively from your vehicle by stopping and using binoculars to scan suitable habitats. It is often more enjoyable to get out, walk slowly and quietly through the area, and use your ears, as well as your eyes, to locate birds. Once you hear a song or see a movement, concentrate on that spot until you can pinpoint the bird with your binoculars and then identify it. Typically birds will quiet down and stop moving around when you first walk into an area, and you may think the area is deserted. Sit down, or stand and wait quietly, and birds may soon surround you as they resume their normal activities.

Attracting Birds

Birds live only where they can satisfy their basic requirements of food, water, cover, and nesting sites. During winter, you can use bird feeders to attract birds to your yard. Most grocery, variety, and feed stores carry a selection of inexpensive feeders along with sunflower seeds and mixed seeds. Place the feeder in an open area near a tree or bush large enough to provide cover for birds and in a spot you can easily see from the house.

By offering sunflower seeds, mixed seeds, suet, and peanut butter in feeders on our front deck, we enjoy birding while going about our daily activities. In summer, we also add sugar-water feeders to attract hummingbirds. As I write this, on a blustery spring morning, I am watching mourning doves, downy woodpeckers, northern flickers, black-billed magpies, mountain chickadees, black-capped chickadees, red-breasted nuthatches, starlings, and house sparrows reduce my suet and seed supply. A brown creeper, attracted by all the activity, is up the trunk of an apple tree searching for insects, and a robin, also attracted by the commotion, is checking the lawn for tasty tidbits.

You can also provide food and attract birds by carefully choosing your landscaping. Plant fruit trees or berry bushes to attract fruit-loving birds, or provide plants with nectar-bearing flowers to entice hummingbirds. Once you have your feeders and plants in place, be patient. It may take the birds days, weeks, or even months to locate these new food sources. When they do, the feeders will attract more birds as time goes on.

Brambling—a rare migrant from Eurasia J. L. WASSINK

You can provide water for the birds with a bird bath, fountain, sprinkler, or by simply creating a puddle. Place your water source where you can see it from the house and away from cover where cats may lie in ambush. Keep the water shallow enough for the birds to walk and bathe in.

Birdhouses make easy nesting sites, but only cavity-nesting species use them. By planting appropriate hedges, shrubs, and trees you can create bird habitat on your property, no matter how small it is. If you provide nesting sites for other birds, you can greatly increase the number of birds around your home. Using these techniques to attract birds, we have observed nearly 70 species on our property over the past seven years, a number that continues to grow with each passing year.

You can tap into a wealth of information on these and other birding activities by joining local or national groups that include birders, such as the Federation of British Columbia Naturalists, the Audubon Society, the National Wildlife Federation, and the American Birding Association. You can also subscribe to various magazines dedicated to birders such as *Birder's World*, *WildBird*, *Bird Watcher's Digest*, and *The Living Bird Quarterly*. These organizations and publications can help you learn how to become a responsible birder, a more knowledgeable birder, and an involved birder. (See the Suggested References for addresses.)

Bird Ecology

Birds exist in a vacuum as an integral part of an ecosystem, one of myriad parts functioning as a whole, with all parts intertwined and working together. To alter a single strand of this web of life affects the entire system. Floods, fires, earthquakes, drought, diseases, insect plagues, and other natural events all contribute to a constantly changing balance of nature. Human activities—farming, logging, mining, road building, stream channelization, fire suppression, suburban sprawl, air and water pollution—throw even more variables into the equation. As these factors alter the conditions on a site, the complement of birds living there also changes.

Broad areas of the Pacific Mountain system share similar climates, elevations, and soil types, resulting in similar communities of plants and animals.

Alpine tundra, found on mountaintops, is easily recognized by its lack of trees. The almost constant, bitterly cold winds freeze-dry any vegetation not insulated by a blanket of snow, preventing its growth. Consequently few woody plants grow there, and the vegetation is primarily low-growing perennials, such as alpine lupine, cinquefoil, alpine aster, and yarrow. Downslope from the alpine tundra, trees such as subalpine fir, western larch, and Engelmann spruce form the subalpine forest. Lower in elevation, on drier, less-severe sites, Douglas fir, ponderosa pine, white fir, quaking aspen, Oregon oak, and lodgepole pine grow in mixed forests. Sagebrush and western juniper occupy the driest areas in the region. The many vegetation types blend with each other, the mix depending on elevation, latitude, slope, aspect, rainfall, and a multitude of other variables.

White-tailed Ptarmigan   J. L. WASSINK

Plant and animal species form a continuum through the region. Some birds, including American robins, have broad environmental adaptability and live almost from mountaintop to sagebrush. You can see them on the alpine tundra in Mount Rainier National Park as well as the dry sagebrush habitats in the lower elevations to the east. Many other species have adapted to survive in specific vegetation types. Knowing a bird's habitat restrictions can help you identify unfamiliar species. The white-tailed ptarmigan, for example, lives primarily on the alpine tundra. When you see a grouselike bird in the sagebrush, you can be sure it is not a ptarmigan.

Within its habitat type, each species of bird has its particular way of living—it feeds, nests, moves, and mates in its unique fashion. While one species of duck feeds in water up to 6 inches deep, another prefers water between 12 and 24 inches deep, and still another seeks out water from 20 to 40 feet deep. Some ducks eat mostly seeds, others mostly vegetation, and still others mostly invertebrates. Ecologists call these individual ways of living "ecological niches." The main description section of each write-up gives information on the bird's niche.

Ethics of Birding

Finding food, defending territories, raising young, migrating, escaping predators, and seeking shelter from the weather make life tenuous at best for wild birds. In our desire to learn more about them and enjoy them, we need to use common sense to avoid disrupting their lives, especially if we threaten their survival.

Birds are individuals and have different levels of tolerance for humans. In general, small birds tolerate more human disturbance than larger species. I have photographed small birds from a few feet away without the aid of a blind and have noticed no change in their behavior. I have also had to remove blinds placed several hundred feet from a nest when the adults exhibited anxiety, and I thought they might abandon their young.

Nesting birds are most susceptible to disturbance early in the nesting cycle. At the egg-laying stage, they may abandon at the slightest disturbance. When you encounter a nest at this stage, leave immediately and watch from a distance. A bird's attachment to its nest increases through incubation and hatching. Just prior to fledging, some individuals will stay with their young no matter what you do. Abandonment is only one problem. Until hatchlings develop feathers, they are incapable of regulating their own body temperature, and the adults must brood the young to keep them warm. If your presence keeps the adults away from the nest too long, exposure to even moderate temperatures may greatly weaken the young. In some cases they will die—without giving you any indication that something was amiss.

You will probably find birding most enjoyable when you can observe the birds going about their normal activities. Agitation, repeated alarm calls, aggressive behavior, or distraction displays are all signs that you are too close. Retreat, or leave if you have to, until the birds calm down. Do not handle eggs or young, and refrain from flattening or cutting protective vegetation around nests. These actions increase the likelihood of nest predation by drawing attention to it either by scent or by exposing it to view. Repeatedly flushing birds from their favored feeding areas can force them to remain in areas with less food, effectively depriving them of needed energy.

Ethical birding is an enjoyable activity, and with care, you can view birds without harming them. It's our responsibility to make sure we do not destroy what we seek to enjoy.

Welcome to the wonderful world of birding!

Cliff Swallow starting nest
J. L. WASSINK

LOONS (order Gaviiformes, family Gaviidae) are large, heavy diving birds. Large webbed feet and legs located well back on their bodies make them strong swimmers but render them almost helpless on land. Consequently they rarely come ashore except while nesting. They dive by leaping forward or simply sinking out of sight, sometimes swimming 50 to 100 yards underwater before resurfacing.

Common Loon   *Gavia immer*

Field marks: 32". Long, flat profile; **black head;** heavy, daggerlike black bill; red eyes; white necklace; **black back densely checkered with small white spots;** yodeling call.

Status: Common migrant and breeding summer resident in BC, on VI, and in northern WA; rare migrant throughout most of the Cascade Range, including NCNP, ONP, MRNP, and CLNP.

With their haunting cry and enchanting behavior, these birds embody the spirit of the wilderness. On their way from their wintering areas on the Pacific coast to their northern breeding grounds, which extend from northern Washington to the Arctic, loons pause to rest and feed at the high mountain lakes of the region. Their distinctive yodel-like wailing laugh often provides the first clue to their presence. Upon their arrival in the north, loons seek out suitable nest sites on the shores of lakes with abundant small fish and crustaceans. The birds' numbers appear to be declining primarily because of disturbance of their nesting areas by boaters.

GREBES (order Podicipediformes, family Podicipedidae) are swimming and diving birds with long necks and inconspicuous tails. Legs set well back on their bodies and lobed toes make them excellent swimmers and clumsy walkers. Grebes feed primarily on fish and small aquatic animals. They engage in elaborate courtship displays accompanied by a variety of wails and whistles before building their floating nests of emergent plants in shallow water near shore. Slight differences in bill size distinguish the sexes. Young grebes often ride on their parents' backs, tucked safely under the wing coverts. Sometimes the young remain there even while the adult dives.

Western Grebe   *Aechmophorus occidentalis*

Field marks: 22". **Long, slim, black and white neck;** long, sharp, green-yellow bill; **black cap extends below the eye.**

Status: Common migrant in extreme southern BC and on VI; locally common breeders in the lower elevations of the region south of the Canadian border; rare in NCNP, ONP, MRNP, CLNP, and BC.

After wintering along the west coast from British Columbia to Mexico, western grebes move inland where they nest in colonies in large, often slightly brackish marshes. Fortunate observers may watch the birds' elaborate courtship display. With heads low and crests erect, the two birds swim toward each other. They dip their beaks into the water and shake their heads vigorously from side to side. Then they turn sideways, raise upright, arch their wings and necks back in a graceful curve, and simultaneously rush over the surface of the water. Suddenly they dive, only to reappear seconds later to swim calmly side by side.

Common Loon   T. J. ULRICH

Western Grebe   J. L. WASSINK

Western Grebe and young   J. L. WASSINK

Horned Grebe
Podiceps auritus

Field marks: 13". Slim shape; sharply pointed bill; **rufous neck: dark head with golden ear tufts extend only to the eyeline.**

Status: Uncommon migrant throughout the region; common migrant and winter resident on VI; local summer resident in BC and northern WA; rare or absent in NCNP, ONP, MRNP, and CLNP.

After wintering along the Pacific coast from Alaska to California, horned grebes often stop over in the Pacific mountain ranges while en route to their northern nesting grounds in western Canada and Alaska. Less gregarious than either the western or eared grebes, horned grebes nest on freshwater marshes, ponds, quiet lakes, and slow-moving rivers.

Eared Grebe
Podiceps nigricollis

Field marks: 13". Slim shape; short, sharply pointed bill; **black head and neck; golden ear tufts extend below the eyeline.**

Status: Fairly common migrant and summer resident east of the Cascade and Coast Range crests, uncommon west of the crests; rare migrant and winter resident on VI; rare in NCNP; uncommon in ONP; absent from MRNP; rare summer resident in CLNP.

Eared grebes nest in colonies on shallow lakes and ponds fringed with cattails and other emergents. They build floating nests over shallow water—often only 8 to 12 inches deep. Unlike the other grebes, they often feed at or near the surface of the water. In contrast to the pied-billed grebes, which escape by disappearing into heavy vegetation, eared grebes head for open water when disturbed. Look for large groups of these gregarious birds throughout the year.

Pied-billed Grebe
Podilymbus podiceps

Field marks: 13". Dull brown, stocky body; **stout, rounded whitish bill with a black ring;** black bib; white undertail coverts.

Status: Fairly common migrant and summer resident of shallow lakes and marshes throughout the lower elevations of the region; uncommon north to VI, very rare farther north; rare resident in NCNP; uncommon summer resident in ONP; accidental in MRNP; absent from CLNP.

This pond-loving grebe prefers water with heavy aquatic vegetation, so it often betrays its presence by its calls—either whinnylike or sounding like *cow-cow-cow*. The specific gravity of a grebe's body is close to that of water, giving it the ability to sink into the water until only its head is exposed and then simply disappear among the cattails when disturbed. Pied-billed grebes feed heavily on invertebrates and so may frequent ponds that lack fish.

Horned Grebe   J. L. WASSINK

Eared Grebe   J. L. WASSINK

Pied-billed Grebe   J. L. WASSINK

PELICANS AND CORMORANTS
(order Pelicaniformes)

Pelicans (family Pelecanidae) are large aquatic fish-eating birds with oversized bills and large gular pouches that they use to catch and carry fish. Large feet with webbing between all 4 toes help propel them through the water.

American White Pelican   *Pelecanus erythrorhynchos*

Field marks: 60". Large; **large flat bill;** large throat patch; white plumage with black wing tips.

Status: An uncommon migrant and local summer resident east of the Cascade and Coast Range crests; very rare in BC and on VI; rare in the west; migrant only in NCNP and CLNP; accidental in ONP; absent from MRNP.

With wings spanning 9½ feet, American white pelicans are the largest birds in the Pacific Coast mountain ranges. Primarily fish eaters, they feed by swimming on the surface of the water by submerging their heads and scooping up fish in their large bills. The large gular pouch expands to contain the catch and up to 3 gallons of water. They press the pouch against their throat to expel the water and then swallow the fish. Groups of pelicans may fish cooperatively by forming a line and herding fish into shallow water. The birds nest in colonies on isolated islands in large lakes or reservoirs primarily east of this region, in the Great Basin, eastern Washington, and central British Columbia. They are rare and erratic breeders within the region. Newly hatched young feed on regurgitated soup. Older youngsters reach into the adults' gullets for partially digested fish. The birds leave the nesting colony for their feeding grounds, which may be 50 miles or more away, in orderly lines, flying low over the water.

Cormorants (family Phalacrocoracidae) are heavy bodied, primarily black birds that swim low in the water with their bill tilted upward. They dive from the surface, sometimes to depths of several hundred feet, and swim underwater in pursuit of fish. They have gular pouches similar to but much smaller than those of the pelicans. The sharply hooked bill enables them to grasp and hold their slippery prey.

Double-crested Cormorant   *Phalacrocorax auritus*

Field marks: 29". Long, low profile on the water; **uplifted head;** hooked bill; orange-yellow throat patch; **glossy black plumage.**

Status: Fairly common summer resident at lower elevations; migrant only in the high mountain lakes; common on the west slope of the Coast Range and on VI; absent from NCNP and MRNP; common year-round resident in ONP; uncommon migrant in CLNP.

The only species of cormorant that ventures inland, the double-crested is the one you are likely to see in this region. These birds are excellent at fishing. Surprisingly, their plumage is not waterproof, and they often perch on offshore rocks or sand bars with their wings half open, drying their feathers. They nest in mixed colonies near lakes and marshes, often with great blue herons. Double-crested cormorants typically choose rocky islands, matted vegetation, and trees to support their nests.

American White Pelican   J. L. WASSINK

American White Pelican   J. L. WASSINK

Double-crested Cormorant   J. L. WASSINK

HERONS, EGRETS, AND BITTERNS
(order Ciconiiformes)

Herons, Egrets, and Bitterns (family Ardeidae) are long-legged
wading birds with long necks and long, straight, daggerlike bills. Most nest in colonies and
develop long plumes, or aigrettes, during the breeding season. They fly with deliberate
wing beats, heads drawn back and legs extended.

Great Blue Heron   *Ardea herodias*

Field marks: 52". **Large;** long yellow bill; **bluish gray color;** black crown stripe
and crest.
Status: Uncommon to common resident throughout much of the region except
in the high mountains; common on VI and in NCNP, ONP, and MRNP;
uncommon in CLNP.

The largest and most visible herons in the area, great blue herons frequent the
shores and shallows of both fresh and salt water and occasionally upland
meadows. They often stand motionless until an unsuspecting fish, frog, or snake
ventures by. In upland meadows, they hunt small rodents in a similar way. They
may also stalk slowly through the shallows, ready to skewer any creature small
enough for them to swallow. Where suitable trees are available, great blue herons
nest in rookeries containing as many as several hundred pairs. They may also nest
on isolated islands.

American Bittern   *Botaurus lentiginosus*

Field marks: 25". Stocky build; moderate size; **black neck stripe; brown
streaked plumage.**
Status: Fairly common summer resident in the lower elevations of the region and
in ONP; uncommon breeding resident on extreme southern BC; rare on VI; absent
from NCNP, MRNP, and CLNP.

This secretive marsh and bog dweller frequents the heavy vegetation bordering
beaver ponds and marshes. Unlike the other herons, which feed mostly in open
water, the solitary bittern prefers to feed among rushes. When startled, it freezes—
neck and beak extended skyward, streaked breast blending beautifully with the
surrounding rushes. Although well camouflaged, it is easy to hear. Its call, a loud,
low pumping noise, is unmistakable as it reverberates through the marsh.

Green-backed Heron   *Butorides striatus*

Field marks: 14". Stocky body; **chestnut head and neck; blue gray crown
and back;** bright orange yellow legs.
Status: Rare and local summer resident in the lower elevations of the region;
uncommon breeding resident in southern BC and on VI; rare in NCNP and ONP;
absent from MRNP and CLNP.

This small, dark heron loves secluded boggy habitats and out-of-the-way
vegetation-clogged backwaters. Uncommon in any season, this heron is the most
acrobatic of the group, even hanging upside down from a perch while spearing
an unwary fish.

Great Blue Heron   J. L. WASSINK

American Bittern   J. L. WASSINK

Green-backed Heron   J. L. WASSINK

SWANS, GEESE, AND DUCKS
(order Anseriformes)

Waterfowl (family Anatidae) are well suited to spending most of their lives on water. Their flat bodies increase buoyancy and their fluffy down insulation wards off the chill of cold water. Long necks allow them to reach deep into the water to feed, and their flattened bills, equipped with toothlike edges called lamellae, enable them to strain tiny food items from the water. With short, powerful legs and webs between their 3 front toes, they move easily through the water. And, when the lakes in the north begin to freeze, their narrow pointed wings carry them to warmer climes far to the south.

Swans (tribe Cygnini), with their pure white plumage, large size, and long necks appear the most impressive of waterfowl. Swans feed by dipping their heads and necks in shallow water in search of plants. Birds living in areas with high concentrations of dissolved iron in the water often have rust stains on their heads and upper necks. The males (cobs) and the females (pens) mate for life and usually raise two young (cygnets) each year.

Trumpeter Swan   *Cygnus buccinator*

Field marks: 65". Large; white plumage; black bill; **best distinguished from the tundra swan by its resonant call.**

Status: Common winter resident west of the Coast Mountains and on VI; uncommon winter resident along the lower Columbia River, Puget Sound, and the Willamette Valley; rare in NCNP and ONP; absent from MRNP and CLNP.

Between 1853 and 1877, Hudson's Bay Company handled more than 17,000 swan skins, a good portion of them trumpeters. The company sold these skins in London for adornments and for use in powder puffs and down garments. Extensive hunting continued until 1933 when only 69 trumpeter swans existed in the lower 48 states—all in the Yellowstone area. The establishment in 1935 of Red Rock Lakes National Wildlife Refuge, with its abundant shallow, slow-moving water preferred by the trumpeter, protected the breeding habitat of these magnificent birds. The population slowly increased until the 1950s, when it reached about 600 birds. Since then, transplants to other areas in the lower 48 states, including some in the Cascades, have helped reestablish breeding populations. The Courtenay River Estuary, near Courtenay on Vancouver Island, is a good place to see up to 2,000 of these birds on their wintering grounds.

Tundra Swan   *Cygnus columbianus*

Field marks: 53". Large; white plumage; black bill, often with a **yellow spot in front of the eye.** Distinguished from trumpeter swan by voice—**call of tundra swan is a high-pitched yelp.**

Status: Winter resident along favored western river bottoms; large migrant flocks at eastern refuges, in BC, and on VI; uncommon in NCNP and ONP; absent from MRNP and CLNP.

Among the earliest spring migrants, large flocks of wintering tundra swans leave their favored feeding areas along the lower Columbia River, the Fraser River Delta, and the Willamette Valley and head north to breed on the arctic tundra. Migrants from farther south pass through the Cascades as late as May. Recently renamed tundra swans to reflect where they breed, these birds were formerly called whistling swans for the sound their powerful wings make during flight.

Trumpeter Swan   J. L. WASSINK

Tundra Swan   J. L. WASSINK

Tundra Swans   J. L. WASSINK

Geese (tribe Anserini) are intermediate in size, weight, and neck length between swans and ducks. Like swans, the sexes look similar, mate for life, and share domestic responsibilities. Having legs set farther forward on their bodies than either swans or the ducks makes geese more mobile on land than those birds, and they often graze and feed on waste grain. Geese migrate in noisy flocks that are difficult to ignore.

Canada Goose
Branta canadensis

Field marks: 36". **Black head and neck; white cheek patch;** brownish black and sides.

Status: Common resident breeder throughout the area; common breeder on VI, in NCNP, and ONP; rare migrant in MRNP; uncommon in CLNP.

The wedge-shaped skeins of "honkers" that grace the autumn skies are known the country over as a sure sign of fall. Canada geese are extremely adaptable birds and are the best known and most widely distributed goose in North America. Their ability to nest anywhere they can find a site relatively protected from predators—on cliffs, in osprey nests, on small islands, atop muskrat mounds, and in a variety of human-made nest structures—has made it possible to introduce breeding populations to many new areas. After the breeding season, the family groups come together in large flocks and spend their nights resting on large rivers, lakes, and reservoirs and their days feeding in nearby fields. Canada geese mate for life, and both parents help raise the young.

Greater White-fronted Goose
Anser albifrons

Field marks: 30". Brown plumage; pink bill; **white face; irregular black markings on chest;** white undertail coverts; pink legs.

Status: Uncommon migrant and winter resident west of the Cascade and Coast range crests and on VI, rare to the east; accidental in NCNP and MRNP; unusual in ONP and CLNP.

Because they migrate by day and rest by night, greater white-fronted geese are not commonly seen in the region except on their wintering grounds along the Pacific coast. They feed and nest near fresh water on the Arctic tundra or taiga.

Snow Goose
Chen caerulescens

Field marks: 29". Small; **all white plumage; rosy pink bill with a black grin patch;** black wing tips; also a rare blue phase with a dark gray body.

Status: Common migrant throughout the area and on the wildlife refuges along the eastern slopes; locally abundant winter resident on VI and the Skagit River Delta of WA; rare migrant and winter resident in NCNP and ONP; accidental in MRNP; absent from CLNP.

The noisiest of the geese, snow geese gather on large marshes where the din of their calling can be heard at great distances. Snow geese seen in this region winter in the marshes of the Skagit River Delta or in the valleys of central California. At Reifel Migratory Bird Sanctuary on Westham Island at the mouth of the Fraser River, up to 40,000 snow geese congregate en route to and from their breeding grounds in northern Canada. They feed on seeds, root stalks, and tubers.

Canada Goose

Greater White-fronted Goose

Snow Goose

Surface Ducks (tribe Anatini), like swans and geese, feed from the surface of

the water by tipping. Limited by their smaller size and shorter necks, they cannot reach as deep into the water as the larger birds and consequently frequent shallow water. Unlike the larger birds, ducks are dimorphic—the males larger and more colorful, the females nondescript. Although experienced birders can easily identify the females, beginners can best recognize them by the company they keep. Both sexes sport a bright patch of color, called a speculum, on their secondary flight feathers. These birds leap vertically into the air from the surface of the water rather than running along the water's surface like other waterfowl. Vegetarians throughout most of the year, they add small mollusks, insects, insect larvae, a variety of other small invertebrates, and small fish to their diet during the nesting season.

Mallard   *Anas platyrhynchos*

Field marks: 16". *Male*–**green head;** white neck ring; chestnut breast; blue speculum. *Female*–mottled brown plumage; **yellowish bill;** blue speculum; whitish tail.
Status: Abundant permanent resident throughout the area, including VI, NCNP, and ONP; occasional migrant and summer resident in MRNP; unusual migrant in CLNP.

The most abundant and familiar duck in this region and on the continent, the mallard is the ancestor of most domestic ducks. Highly adaptable, mallards make themselves at home wherever they find suitable shallow water. These hardy birds can endure fierce cold, needing only open water and food to survive. Where some degree of protection accompanies suitable habitat, such as in city parks and other preserves, populations can expand to the point of becoming a problem.

Like other dabbling ducks, mallards feed on the surface of shallow water or on the bottom by reaching down from the surface by "tipping" up in the water. They may make occasional shallow dives to reach tidbits in slightly deeper water.

Pair bonds are established, beginning in late fall and through the winter. Reconnaissance flights over suitable habitat play a part in the selection of the nest site. Once they choose the site, the pair builds a nest, and the female begins laying her eggs. As incubation proceeds, the pair bond begins to dissolve and eventually the drake moves to a nearby marsh, where he joins other males and undergoes his annual molt.

Gadwall   *Anas strepera*

Field marks: 20". *Male*–**gray plumage; black rump;** white speculum. *Female*–mottled brown plumage; unspotted orange bill; white speculum.
Status: Uncommon to abundant migrant and common resident throughout the area, especially at the lower elevations; common winter resident on southern VI; rare resident breeder in NCNP; rare in ONP; absent from CLNP and MRNP.

Less colorful than many of the other ducks, gadwalls are easily overlooked. More prone to dive than the other dabbling ducks, they seem to prefer stagnant sloughs where they feed on aquatic vegetation. They are also excellent walkers and often feed in woodlands and grain fields. Populations of gadwalls seem to be increasing, and they are gradually extending their range toward the eastern parts of this region.

Mallard pair   J. L. WASSINK

Mallard pair tipping   J. L. WASSINK

Gadwall drake   J. L. WASSINK

Northern Pintail
Anas acuta

Field marks: 25". Slim shape. *Male*–brown head; **vertical white chest and neck stripe; long pointed tail;** black rump. *Female*–brown plumage; long neck; long tail.

Status: Common to abundant migrant and fairly common breeding resident throughout the region; rare breeder on VI and in NCNP; common winter resident in ONP; rare migrant in MRNP and CLNP.

Early migrants, these long, slender, graceful fliers can be seen in tight flocks wheeling and gliding over marshes or grain fields. They often feed on dry land and may nest well away from water. When feeding in water, their long necks allow them to reach greater depths than the other surface ducks, and so they do less tipping. They head south in August, before the hot days of summer are over. Pintails are one of the most abundant North American ducks, outnumbered only by the mallard and possibly the lesser scaup.

American Wigeon
Anas americana

Field marks: 19". *Male*–**white crown; green eye patch;** brown back; green speculum; **white upper wing coverts** visible in flight. *Female*–streaked brown; black speculum; **white upper wing coverts** visible in flight.

Status: Abundant migrant and rare to common summer resident in the lower elevations of the region; common migrant and winter resident on VI; rare migrant and summer resident in NCNP; common winter resident in ONP; absent from CLNP and MRNP.

More vegetarian than other ducks, wigeon prefer open marshes and lakes with aquatic vegetation near the surface. Their love of grazing often brings them to urban parks and golf courses during the winter months. Also called "baldpate," wigeon are social ducks that often associate with gadwalls. Prior to nesting, spring courtship brings sharp whistling calls and frequent aerial chases. In winter, wigeon keep company with large rafts of diving ducks. There, in addition to seeking out their own food, wigeon engage in piracy. While the divers go down after tasty morsels, the wigeon wait on the surface. When a diver surfaces with a snack, one of the wigeon grabs it, eats it, and waits for the opportunity to pirate another bite.

Eurasian Wigeon
Anas penelope

Field marks: 18". *Male*–**cream-colored forehead;** rusty brown head; gray flanks. *Female*–similar to female American wigeon.

Status: Rare migrant throughout the region, including VI; absent from NCNP, MRNP, and CLNP; rare winter resident in ONP.

Common in Europe, these birds usually visit this region as lone birds in flocks of American wigeon. Although they are seen frequently, especially along the coasts, we have no records of them breeding in this country. The habits and ecology of the European wigeon are virtually identical to those of the American wigeon.

Northern Pintail drake and Northern Pintail hen (*inset*)   J. L. WASSINK

American Wigeon   J. L. WASSINK

Eurasian Wigeon   J. L. WASSINK

Northern Shoveler
Anas clypeata

Field marks: 19". *Male*–**large spatulate bill; green head;** rusty sides; white chest; **pale blue upper wing coverts.** *Female*–**large spatulate bill;** mottled brown plumage.

Status: Abundant migrant and rare to common summer resident in the lower elevations of the region and on VI; rare in upper elevations and in NCNP; rare resident in ONP; absent from MRNP and CLNP.

Shovelers feed on tiny invertebrates in very shallow water. Taking a billful of bottom ooze, the shoveler swishes its bill from side to side, forcing out water and liquid mud between the comblike lamellae on the edges of the bill and leaving behind insect larvae, small crustaceans, seeds, and bits of plant material. Other times it may swim slowly, with its neck extended, and use its bill to skim insects of the surface of the water. If suitable shallows are unavailable, shovelers will also tip to feed like the other surface ducks.

Blue-winged Teal
Anas discors

Field marks: 15". *Male*–**small;** slate gray head; **white crescent in front of eye;** green speculum; **pale blue upper wing coverts.** *Female*–brown plumage; pale spot behind bill; pale blue upper wing coverts.

Status: Uncommon migrant and summer resident east of the Cascade and Coast range crests, more common to the west and on VI; rare in NCNP and ONP; absent from MRNP and CLNP.

Long-distance migrants that winter as far away as Central America, blue-winged teal are one of the last ducks to arrive in spring and the first to head south in autumn. Upon arrival, they seek out small shallow grassy marshes, where they stick close to shore, feeding on aquatic plants in the shallows and resting on the shore. Skilled fliers, they resemble squadrons of fighter planes on maneuvers in tight formation, gliding just above the marsh vegetation.

Cinnamon Teal
Anas cyanoptera

Field marks: 15". *Male*–small; **cinnamon-colored plumage;** red eyes; **pale blue upper wing coverts.** *Female*–brown plumage; large, broad bill; no whitish spot behind bill like the female blue-winged teal.

Status: Rare to common migrant and fairly common summer resident east of the Cascade and Coast range crests; rare in NCNP and to the west and on VI; rare breeding resident in ONP; absent from MRNP and CLNP.

Like the blue-winged teal, the cinnamon teal inhabits small, shallow, grassy marshes. But, it tends to choose drier or more alkaline areas than the blue-winged teal does and replaces them in these habitats. Cinnamon teal usually form smaller flocks than other teal. They feed on aquatic plants in shallow water, along the water's edge or on mudflats, and they nest on land, hidden in dense vegetation.

Northern Shoveler   J. L. WASSINK

Blue-winged Teal pair   J. L. WASSINK

Cinnamon Teal   J. L. WASSINK

Green-winged Teal
Anas crecca

Field marks: 14". *Male*–small; **chestnut head with a green patch from the eye to the nape; white vertical stripe up side of breast.** *Female*–brown plumage; white belly; green speculum
Status: Abundant winter resident, abundant migrant, and uncommon to common summer resident at lower elevations, on VI, and in ONP; rare in NCNP; occasional in MRNP; absent from CLNP.

The smallest of the North American dabbling ducks, the green-winged teal is one of the ducks that winters in this region. They prefer marshy, weedy river bottoms or wooded sloughs. Flocks of these agile birds fly swiftly, wheeling and dipping over the small ponds they often frequent. The female builds her nest in tall vegetation near the water and lays between 10 and 12 eggs.

Wood Duck
Aix sponsa

Field marks: 13". *Male*–**red eye and bill; green head with striped crest; burgundy chest; white belly;** buff sides; long tail. *Female*–**gray head and crest; white eye patch;** brownish gray sides; white belly.
Status: Common breeding summer resident throughout the region and on southern VI; rare breeder in NCNP and in ONP; accidental in MRNP; rare summer visitor in CLNP.

Wood ducks inhabit calm waters of swamps, ponds, lakes, streams, and wooded backwaters. They nest in tree cavities and were adversely affected by logging and thinning within their marshy habitats. In recent years, many people have put out nest boxes for these colorful birds, and their numbers have increased. Usually found in pairs or in small flocks, wood ducks may gather in large groups during fall and winter. They ride higher in the water than most ducks and commonly swim with their tail at 45 degrees above horizontal. Most wood ducks go south with the coming of winter, but a few may remain in isolated pockets of freshwater.

Green–winged Teal pair J. L. WASSINK

Wood Duck drake J. L. WASSINK

Wood Duck hen J. L. WASSINK

Bay Ducks or Diving Ducks (tribe Aythyini), as the two

designations imply, are ducks that prefer the open areas of fairly large, deep bodies of water and feed by diving. They winter in bays along both coasts and the Gulf of Mexico, but move to inland marshes in spring to nest. Unlike the surface ducks, who build their nests on land, divers build their nests over water. Diving ducks take flight by running across the surface of the water until they gain enough momentum to become airborne. Their larger feet, lobed hind toe, and legs set farther back on their bodies make them more powerful swimmers than the surface ducks but more awkward on land.

Redhead   *Aythya americana*

Field marks: 19". *Male*–**rusty red head; dish-faced profile;** black breast and rump; **gray back and sides.** *Female*–brown plumage; round head; white belly.
Status: Rare in the region except for sizeable breeding populations on some of the refuges east of the Cascade crest; rare on VI and in NCNP and ONP; absent from MRNP and CLNP.

Redheads arrive in fast-moving Vs to rest and feed on their way north to the prairie potholes where most of them breed. The draining of nesting ponds has permanently reduced the numbers of these and other pothole-nesting ducks. Redhead females seem rather careless with their eggs, laying them in the nests of other species as well as constructing "dump" nests where several redhead females lay eggs but don't incubate them. The females also build their own nests and raise a clutch of their own. More vegetarian than other divers, redheads like shallow lakes and marshes where they dive to depths of about 10 feet in pursuit of pondweed, their favorite food. In winter, redheads keep company with other diving ducks, particularly scaup.

Canvasback   *Aythya valisineria*

Field marks: 20". *Male*–**long sloping forehead;** chestnut red head; **white back and sides.** *Female*–**long sloping forehead;** brown plumage.
Status: Occasional to uncommon migrant but rare breeder in the lower elevations of this region; migrant only on VI; rare breeder in NCNP; rare in ONP; absent from MRNP; rare summer visitor in CLNP.

One of the largest of the diving ducks, "cans"—as hunters affectionately call them—are largely vegetarian. Capable of diving to 30 feet, they most often feed on the tuberous roots of aquatic plants found in 3 to 15 feet of water. Favored foods are wapatoo and pondweed. After breeding in the emergent vegetation surrounding small ponds and lakes, canvasbacks congregate in great numbers on large lakes and reservoirs. Long, pointed wings carry these powerful fliers at speeds up to 60 miles per hour. Like many of the pothole-nesting ducks, canvasbacks do not breed in drought years when their nesting ponds dry up. Canvasbacks typically winter on coastal bays, where they often fall victim to food-thieving coots and wigeon.

Redhead drake   J. L. WASSINK

Redhead hen   J. L. WASSINK

Canvasback drake   J. L. WASSINK

Ring-necked Duck

Aythya collaris

Field marks: 12". *Male*–**dark head, neck, and breast** with purple sheen; **white band on bill; black back;** gray sides. *Female*–gray brown plumage; gray bill with black tip and white ring; pale eye ring; steep forehead; peaked crown.

Status: Fairly common migrant and winter resident but rare breeder in this region and on VI; uncommon in NCNP and ONP; absent from MRNP or CLNP.

Woodland ponds ringed with stubbly growth provide the preferred habitat of the ring-necked duck. These ducks build their nests in boggy or marshy areas rather than on dry land. Although they can dive to 40 feet, they prefer to feed in water from 2 to 5 feet deep, where they hunt for tubers, pondweed, and seeds. In even shallower water, they will "tip" like the dabblers. Ring-necked ducks pass through this region late in the spring on their way to the reedy borders of bogs and ponds of northern Washington and southern Canada. These gregarious ducks form sizeable flocks during migration and then gather on large lakes and tidal estuaries along the Pacific coast to spend the winter. Unlike many divers, ring-necked ducks are rarely seen on salt water and seldom mingle with other species.

Greater Scaup

Aythya marila

Field marks: 13". *Male*–pale blue bill with dark tail; dark head, neck and breast with a greenish sheen; **rounded head profile;** pale gray back and sides; black rump. *Female*–brown plumage.

Status: Common migrant and winter resident on saltwater bays and estuaries, on VI, and in ONP; rare in NCNP; absent from MRNP and CLNP.

Greater scaup winter in flocks, often numbering in the thousands, on open bays or out on the open ocean where they dive for mollusks. From there, they migrate through the Cascades on their way to their nesting grounds across northern Canada.

Lesser Scaup

Aythya affinis

Field marks: 12". *Male*–pale blue bill with dark nail; dark head, neck and breast with a purple sheen; **peaked head profile;** barred gray back and sides; black rump. *Female*–brown plumage.

Status: Common migrant and winter resident along the coast south from VI and southern BC; rare breeder in northern WA; rare summer visitor in NCNP and ONP; absent from MRNP; rare year-round in CLNP.

Like the greater scaup, lesser scaup congregate along the Pacific coast in winter. However, they prefer the less salty water of brackish bays and deep, freshwater reservoirs and lakes where they feed almost exclusively on aquatic invertebrates. Scaup are expert divers. In fall they linger in the north anywhere they find open water until forced to move south as the water freezes. Scaup nest late, and the young often do not hatch until July.

Ring-necked Duck drake T. J. ULRICH

Greater Scaup R. BEHRSTOCK, VIREO

Lesser Scaup drake J. L. WASSINK

Common Goldeneye

Bucephala clangula

Field marks: 18". *Male*–glossy green head; **yellow eye; white round face spot;** mostly white body. *Female*–mostly gray body; brown head; **yellow eye.**

Status: Common migrant and winter resident throughout this region, on VI, and in ONP; uncommon migrant and winter resident in NCNP; absent from MRNP; rare migrant in CLNP.

The last migrants to pass through this region in the fall, common goldeneye winter wherever the water remains open, typically on large reservoirs or rivers. Goldeneye are usually found in loose association with other goldeneye. These expert divers commonly feed by turning over underwater debris and stones in search of crabs and other crustaceans. Their flight is swift and produces a whistling sound— thus the nickname "whistler." Cavity nesters, goldeneye nest in forested habitat where large trees provide the necessary hollows. After hatching, the chicks launch themselves out of the nest into the air and bounce unhurt off the ground.

Barrow's Goldeneye

Bucephala islandica

Field marks: 18". *Male*–purple gloss on head; **crescent-shaped face spot;** more **black on the sides** than common goldeneye. *Female*–similar to the female common goldeneye but with an **all-yellow bill.**

Status: Locally common migrant and winter resident and rare breeder along both slopes of the Cascades and on VI; uncommon resident in NCNP and ONP; occasional migrant and summer visitor in MRNP; rare migrant and summer visitor in CLNP.

Like common goldeneye, Barrow's goldeneye winter as far north as they can find open water. Also like the common goldeneye, these birds nest in old woodpecker holes and abandoned squirrel dens near mountain lakes, ponds, and rivers. Although small fish provide most of their diet, they also take some invertebrates and bits of vegetation. During nesting, Barrow's goldeneye commonly eat insects.

Bufflehead

Bucephala albeola

Field marks: 14". *Male*–**small;** mostly white plumage; dark iridescent head with a **wedge-shaped white patch.** *Female*–small; gray-brown plumage; **light patch below and behind the eye.**

Status: Common migrant and winter resident but rare summer resident throughout the region, on VI, and in ONP; uncommon breeder in NCNP; accidental in MRNP; absent from CLNP.

The smallest of the divers, the diminutive bufflehead is a perky little duck that seems to be in constant motion. Unlike other diving ducks, it can leap directly out of the water like a puddle duck when disturbed. The female usually selects an old flicker hole in which to lay her eggs. Upon hatching, the young have only one way to reach the ground—jump—which they do, landing unharmed. Like most of the ducks in this region, buffleheads winter in nearby waters along the Pacific coast.

Common Goldeneye pair   J. L. WASSINK

Male Barrow's Goldeneye   T. J. ULRICH

Bufflehead drake   J. L. WASSINK

Harlequin Duck

Histrionicus histrionicus

Field marks: 12". *Male*–gray blue bill; **gray blue head with white crescent in front of eye and white spots on sides of head;** gray blue back; white marking in front of wing; chestnut sides. *Female*–gray blue bill; **dark gray brown head with three white spots**; dark gray brown body.
Status: Uncommon resident of high turbulent mountain rivers in BC, WA, and northern OR; less common farther south; uncommon breeder on VI and in NCNP; common resident in ONP; occasional breeder in MRNP; absent from CLNP.

Uncommon and shy, harlequin ducks spend their winters in the heavy surf along the Pacific coast from the Aleutians to central California. With the coming of spring, they venture inland and seek out swift, cold, turbulent rivers. They feed by diving to pick caddis fly larvae and other invertebrates from the river's rocky bottom. Quite agile on land, the female chooses a nest site among streamside rocks or deadfall. Soon after the eggs are laid, the male flies back to the coast, leaving the female to raise the young.

White-winged Scoter

Melanitta fusca

Field marks: 16". *Male*–reddish orange bill with dark protuberance at the base; **dark overall; small white comma below eye; white speculum.** *Female*–**dark bill; dark overall; two pale white spots on side of head, white speculum.**
Status: Common summer resident east of the Coast Range of BC and a common migrant on VI and in the northern part of the Cascades; rare migrant in NCNP; common winter resident and uncommon summer resident in ONP; accidental in MRNP; absent from CLNP.

The largest of the three scoters of the region, the white-winged scoter is also the one most likely to be found inland. It congregates in mixed flocks, and in winter great flocks ride the water in tight formation in protected coves from the Aleutians to Baja. Solitary white-winged scoters may occasionally be seen on large freshwater lakes or reservoirs where, as elsewhere, they feed mainly by diving for invertebrates and other small animal life.

Ruddy Duck

Oxyura jamaicensis

Field marks: 15". *Male*–deep rusty red body; **bright blue bill;** black cap; white cheeks; **long tail often carried pointing straight up.** *Female*–brownish color; whitish cheek patch; **long, often upturned tail.**
Status: Common migrant throughout the region; fairly common summer resident on the east slopes; less common in the west; absent from NCNP and MRNP; uncommon winter resident on VI and in ONP; rare in CLNP.

Most common at lower elevations, ruddy ducks breed in ponds and lakes overgrown with vegetation and ringed with cattails or bulrushes. There the male performs his unique courtship routine of beating his bill on his breast and producing a thumping-gurgling sound. The females lay unusually large eggs and commonly drop them in the nests of other ducks. Like most diving ducks, ruddys winter in nearby protected coastal bays, where they raft with other diving ducks.

Harlequin Duck pair   J. L. WASSINK

Male White-winged Scoter   ARTHUR MORRIS, VISUALS UNLIMITED

Ruddy Duck drake   J. L. WASSINK

Hooded Merganser
Lophodytes cucullatus

Field marks: 13". *Male*–**thin black bill; dark head with white crest;** black back; white breast; rusty flanks; white speculum. *Female*–**thin black orange bill; brown head with orange rust crest;** dark back; gray brown breast and sides; white speculum.

Status: Fairly common migrant and breeder on VI and in southern Coast Mountains; fairly common resident breeder in Washington; less common farther south; rare breeding resident in NCNP and ONP; accidental in MRNP; rare summer visitor in CLNP.

Hooded mergansers, the smallest of the three mergansers in the region, frequent many of the habitats preferred by wood ducks: brushy margins of rivers, streams, ponds, and lakes. However, hooded mergansers also use faster streams and rivers not favored by wood ducks. The similarities between the two birds continue: They both nest in tree cavities and adapt readily to nest boxes; their young leave the nest by climbing to the opening, launching themselves into the air, and bouncing to the ground. Like wood ducks, and quite unlike the other mergansers, hooded mergansers take flight by leaping directly into the air and are at home on land. Their food choices, however, differ greatly from those of wood ducks; hooded mergansers use their slim serrated bills to capture fish and other small animals found in their home waters.

Common Merganser
Mergus merganser

Field marks: 24". *Male*–long, low profile; black above; white below; **long, slender, hooked red bill; green head;** red legs. *Female*–**dark chestnut head;** gray plumage; **clear white throat.**

Status: Common migrant and winter resident throughout the region; uncommon breeding resident in NCNP; common breeding resident on VI and in ONP; rare migrant and breeding summer resident in MRNP; common resident in CLNP.

Much larger than hooded mergansers, common mergansers prefer larger and more open streams and marshy bays within the boreal forest. They search out nearby hollow trees or similarly well-protected cavities to protect their nests. This adept swimmer feeds almost exclusively on small fish, locating them either by snorkeling (swimming with only the bill and eyes submerged) or by diving. Its slender saw-toothed bill, source of its nickname "sawbill," is perfect for grasping slippery prey. When flushed, common mergansers must make a long exhausting run across the surface of the water to gain enough speed to become airborne. Common during winter, these birds move north and inland as the ice disappears, and so are seldom seen here in summer. The similar red-breasted merganser has a more northerly distribution, frequents salt water more often than the common merganser does, and has a wispy crest, a white neck, and a reddish breast.

Hooded Merganser displaying   J. L. WASSINK

Common Merganser drake   J. L. WASSINK

Common Merganser drakes displaying to hen   J. L. WASSINK

VULTURES, HAWKS, EAGLES, AND FALCONS

(order Falconiformes) are diurnal birds of prey that feed on flesh. Most of these birds have strong legs and feet tipped with long, curved talons designed for grasping and killing prey and strong, heavy, hooked beaks for tearing it into pieces. A few members of this family are scavengers. In most species, the females are larger but otherwise similar to the males.

Vultures (family Cathartidae) use their broad wings to soar effortlessly for hours on rising thermals. The naked heads of these large, dark scavengers stay cleaner than feathered heads would.

Turkey Vulture   *Cathartes aura*

> **Field marks:** 29". Black body; small naked reddish head. *In flight*–**uptilted wings;** wings black in front, gray behind.
> **Status:** Regularly seen south of the Canadian border except in winter; accidental in the Coast Mountains of BC; uncommon migrant and summer visitor on VI and in NCNP and ONP; accidental in MRNP; uncommon migrant and summer visitor in CLNP.

Look for turkey vultures high overhead, circling effortlessly on uptilted wings as they ride rising thermals. Scavengers with keen eyes and a well-developed sense of smell, vultures locate carrion either by sight or by smell. Almost as soon as the first bird drops from the sky, more appear out of nowhere to join in the meal. Once on the ground, they struggle to become airborne once again. More common at low elevations, turkey vultures nest in crevices or under overhangs on inaccessible cliffs. They feed their 1 or 2 youngsters regurgitated carrion.

Hawks and Eagles (family Accipitridae) are all excellent fliers with

strong legs and powerful talons. They lack the characteristic notch in the beak common to the falcons.

Accipiters are small to medium-sized hawks that hunt in heavy woodlands and feed mainly on birds. Short, rounded wings and long tails give them the speed and maneuverability to pursue small birds through dense woods. In open flight, they alternate flapping and gliding. Females are generally larger than males.

Sharp-shinned Hawk   *Accipiter striatus*

> **Field marks:** *Male*–11"; *female*–13". Small; short, rounded wings; long, **square tipped tail**; dark gray above; white with rust bars below.
> **Status:** Uncommon breeding resident in southern BC, VI, and south through the Cascades, including NCNP and ONP; uncommon migrant in MRNP; uncommon summer visitor in CLNP; summer visitor only in Coast Mountains of BC.

The sharp-shinned hawk is the smallest and most common of the three North American accipiter hawks. It hunts by flashing through the trees, flushing its prey, and then snatching the fleeing victim out of midair. Occasionally, the hawk will be so intent on pursuing its prey that it will crash headlong into a thicket or a tree branch. Once caught the prey is taken to a favorite perch, called a butcher block, plucked, and eaten. Sharp-shinned hawks also take some insects and small mammals, usually mice. Although the similar Cooper's hawk has a round-tipped tail and is slightly larger (14" to 20"), the species are almost indistinguishable.

Turkey Vulture   J. L. WASSINK

Turkey Vulture   J. L. WASSINK

Sharp-shinned Hawk   J. L. WASSINK

Harriers are slim hawks with long, rounded wings and long tails. They hold their wings above horizontal while gliding low over the ground to hunt.

Northern Harrier   *Circus cyaneus*

Field marks: *Male*–18"; slim shape; **silvery gray.** *Female*–22"; slim; **dark brown.** *In flight*–**long, narrow uplifted wings; white rump;** flies low over the ground; sometimes hovers.
Status: Uncommon migrant and summer resident in the southern Coast Mountains and on VI; fairly common resident in suitable habitats of the Cascades and in ONP; uncommon migrant in NCNP; uncommon summer visitor in MRNP; rare summer visitor in CLNP.

Look for "marsh hawks" flying buoyantly through open country, usually quartering low over marshy habitat in search of mice, voles, frogs, or snakes. Facial disks, similar to those of owls, focus sound and enable northern harriers to locate prey by sound as well as by sight—a useful ability in the tall grass habitats they patrol. Northern harriers nest in marshes, building their nests just above the water. The male brings food to the female during incubation and early during the brooding. The female, always alert, sees him coming and leaves the nest to meet him. He drops the food item; she catches it in midair and immediately returns to the nest. Marsh hawks move south for the winter, spending the cold months from the southern part of this region down to South America.

Buteos are medium to large soaring hawks of open country. Consequently, their wings are broad and round, and their tails are broad and fan shaped. They locate prey from high overhead and pursue it from a steep dive. Several of these species have two color phases, one dark and one light, which complicates identification.

Red-tailed Hawk   *Buteo jamaicensis*

Field marks: 21". *In flight*–**rusty tail**; long broad wings; wings whitish except for dark leading edge from body to "wrist"; round tail. *Perched*–white breast; dark head and back.
Status: Uncommon resident in southern Coast Mountains and on VI; common resident throughout most of the Cascades; common resident in NCNP and ONP; common breeder and summer resident in MRNP; uncommon summer resident in CLNP.

Its adaptability has made the red-tailed hawk the most common hawk in the region. It feeds primarily on rodents and rabbits but will also take birds, snakes, frogs, and virtually anything else it can catch—even rattlesnakes. This raptor usually builds its bulky nest in a large tree but, in open country, will nest on cliffs. Red-tailed hawks winter in the southern states along the Gulf of Mexico but return to the same nest year after year. Because of its predatory habits, the red-tail has suffered from persecution by humans intent on protecting their domestic animals.

Male Northern Harrier   T. J. ULRICH

Red-tailed Hawk   B. K. WHEELER, VIREO

Red-tailed Hawk   T. J. ULRICH

Rough-legged Hawk

Buteo lagopus

Field marks: 23". Species has both a light phase and a dark phase, as well as intermediate colors. The following are generally true for all color phases: *In flight–* **white base of tail; dark "wrist" marks on underwings.** *Perching–*brownish above with light edges on feathers; white base of tail; dark belly.

Status: Rare to uncommon migrant and winter resident in the open habitats of the region south of the middle of the Coast Mountains and VI; rare migrant in NCNP and in ONP; common fall migrant in MRNP; rare migrant and summer visitor in CLNP.

After breeding in the Arctic and subarctic, rough-legged hawks move south in search of more abundant prey. Preferring more open country than the red-tailed hawk, rough-legged hawks typically perch on roadside power poles or hover low while searching the ground below for the telltale movement of a small rodent. The widely fluctuating numbers of rough-legged hawks wintering in the region are believed to be linked to populations of lemmings, a favorite prey, farther north.

Ospreys are hawks that live exclusively on fish. This family contains only one species.

Osprey

Pandion haliaetus

Field marks: 24". Predominantly white; broad, black cheek line; black back. *In flight–*long white wings bent at the "wrist"; **black "wrist" markings.**

Status: Uncommon summer resident throughout the region; uncommon summer resident on VI and in NCNP; common summer resident in ONP; rare summer visitor in MRNP; uncommon summer visitor in CLNP.

Ospreys live along clear mountain lakes and streams where fish are plentiful. They spot fish from the air, then dive talons-first into the water to nab their catch. A reversible outer toe and spiny pads, called spicules, on the bottoms of their feet give them a better grip on their slippery prey. Ospreys carry fish, with the head turned forward, either to a perch to eat or to the nest to feed the young. These "fish hawks" build bulky nests near water in tall trees, on power poles, or more recently, on nesting platforms provided by concerned utility companies. Ospreys will use the same nests year after year. Once decimated by DDT, populations of these birds are increasing once again.

Rough-legged Hawk   J. L. WASSINK

Osprey   J. L. WASSINK

Osprey   J. L. WASSINK

Golden Eagle

Aquila chrysaetos

Field marks: 35". *Adults*–**large;** dark plumage; **golden cast to hind neck;** fully feathered tarsus; *in flight*–large size; dark plumage; large broad wings. *Immature*–dark plumage with some white spots; *in flight*–dark plumage; white "wrist" spots; white in tail but tip black.

Status: Rare to uncommon resident east of the Cascade and Coast range crests; even less common on the west slope; rare to uncommon breeding resident on VI and in NCNP and ONP; uncommon to common summer resident in MRNP; rare resident in CLNP.

The largest raptors in the Pacific mountain ranges, golden eagles are birds of the mountains. They prefer open country: alpine meadows, mountain ridges, grasslands, sagebrush plateaus, piñon-juniper slopes, and semi-desert canyons. From high overhead, soaring on set wings, they search the ground for any movement that betrays the presence of prey—mammals, including ground squirrels, rabbits, and marmots, and birds, including ring-necked pheasants and chukars. Upon spotting prey, an eagle pursues the unsuspecting creature with a long swift silent dive, then clenches the victim in its powerful talons. Some accuse golden eagles of stealing lambs, which they rarely do. Persecution by humans, pesticide contamination, and elimination of its prey by habitat destruction limit the golden eagle's population. Golden eagles mate for life, nest in trees or on cliffs, and raise one or two chicks per year.

Bald Eagle

Haliaeetus leucocephalus

Field marks: 36". *Adults*–dark plumage; **white head and tail; heavy yellow bill.** *Immature*–dark plumage. *In flight*–underwing coverts lighter than flight feathers.

Status: Rare to fairly common resident in the region; rare resident and common winter visitor in NCNP; common resident on VI and in ONP; occasional to rare migrant and summer visitor in MRNP; uncommon to rare resident in CLNP.

Our national symbol, the bald eagle feeds mostly on fish, waterfowl, and carrion. It nests near fertile lakes and rivers that support an abundance of nongame fish, such as suckers and squawfish, which it snatches from the surface of the water with its sharp talons. Bald eagles also feed on waterfowl, rodents, and carrion found near water. Not above piracy, they will harry a fish-laden osprey into dropping its booty, which the eagle snags out of midair. This eagle builds its nests in tall trees near water. Bald eagles pair for life and return to the same territory year after year. Pair bonds are renewed each year with spectacular courtship displays, including locked-talon cartwheels that begin high in the air and spin toward the earth with breathtaking speed. The pair raises 2 young each year if the food supply is adequate. The white plumage on the head of the adult bird appears at about 3 to 5 years of age. Threatened by DDT contamination of its food supply, the bald eagle is recovering.

Golden Eagle on deer kill   T. J. ULRICH

Immature Bald Eagle   J. L. WASSINK   **Bald Eagle**   J. L. WASSINK

Falcons (family Falconidae), with their notched beaks, long pointed wings, and long slender tails are strong, fast fliers. These streamlined birds inhabit open country and locate their prey from a prominent perch or from a vantage point high in the air, then overtake it in a long, steep dive.

Prairie Falcon
Falco mexicanus

Field marks: 16". Medium size; pale brown above; light below in flight; pointed wings; quick wingbeats; **"black armpits."**

Status: Occasional in lowlands west of the Cascade crest; more common in areas with cliffs near open country on the east side; rare on VI; rare migrant and summer resident in NCNP; rare migrant in ONP and MRNP; uncommon breeding resident in CLNP.

Prairie falcons inhabit dry sagebrush-covered semi-desert and plains. They hunt mainly ground squirrels but will take birds, reptiles, and even insects. After spotting their prey, prairie falcons "stoop," or dive, at speeds approaching 200 miles per hour. They build no nest, but lay their eggs in a scrape on a protected ledge on the face of a cliff. They warn intruders with a *kik-kik-kik*.

Peregrine Falcon
Falco peregrinus

Field marks: 18". Dark above; light below; **dark "mustache."** *In flight*–medium size; lacks the dark "armpits" of the prairie falcon.

Status: Rare and endangered resident throughout the region; rare summer resident in NCNP; common breeding resident in ONP; rare winter visitor in MRNP; rare breeding resident on VI and in CLNP.

The widespread use of pesticides has extirpated this species from much of its former range. The peregrine falcon nests on cliffs, usually overlooking water, and hunts mainly birds—waterfowl, shorebirds, and songbirds. Capable of stooping at speeds exceeding 200 miles per hour, it is our fastest bird. Specialized baffles in the nostrils allow it to breathe during the stoop. A peregrine kills its prey by overtaking it in midair and either striking it with a fisted foot or by grasping it with sharp talons. Efforts are currently under way to reintroduce the peregrine falcon to its historic range. Peregrines have reoccupied some or their traditional eyries, or nesting sites, suggesting the efforts are at least partially successful.

American Kestrel
Falco sparverius

Field marks: 8". **Small; rusty back and tail with black bars;** "mustache"; pointed wings. *Male*–bluish wings; *female*–brown wings and tail.

Status: Uncommon to common summer resident throughout the region; uncommon summer resident on VI and in NCNP and ONP; common summer resident in MRNP; uncommon migrant and common summer resident in CLNP.

The smallest and most widespread falcon, the American kestrel feeds mostly on insects but also takes mice, frogs, and small birds. It prefers open country, where it hunts from its perch on a telephone wire or while hovering in the air. American kestrels nest in tree cavities, old woodpecker holes, in crevices, or in buildings. Warning call is *killy-killy-killy*.

Prairie Falcon   J. L. WASSINK

Peregrine Falcon   J. L. WASSINK

Female American Kestrel   J. L. WASSINK

Male American Kestrel   J. L. WASSINK

TURKEYS, GROUSE, QUAIL, PHEASANTS, PARTRIDGES, AND PTARMIGAN (order Galliformes) are

heavy-bodied, chickenlike land birds. Their short, heavy bills have a decurved upper mandible, ideal for foraging on seeds and insects. They rely heavily on their powerful legs to carry them out of danger—their short rounded wings enable them to attain full flight speed with a couple wing beats but do not allow sustained flight. The males are more colorful than the females and engage in elaborate courtship displays. The courting males will strut; raise or spread specialized feathers on the head, neck, or tail; inflate air sacs in the neck; beat the air with their wings, or release air from sacs to produce a variety of courtship sounds. They nest on the ground and lay large clutches of 10 to 14 eggs. The young hatch covered with down and leave the nest almost immediately.

Turkeys (family Phasianidae, subfamily Meleagrididae) are large birds with naked

heads, broad wings, long legs, and broad fan-shaped tails. They feed primarily on nuts and seeds.

Wild Turkey   *Meleagris gallopavo*

> **Field marks:** *Male*–48"; *female*–36". **Large;** dark iridescent plumage; large fan-shaped tail tipped with buff; **naked head.**
> **Status:** Local as a result of introductions on VI, and in central Washington and north-central Oregon; absent from BC and the region's national parks.

Wild turkeys reside in ponderosa pine forests or mixed woods along streams and rivers of the region. They move in flocks except when the hens scatter to nest in the spring. During courtship, the males spread their long, broad, colorful tails and strut and gobble—a habit that often betrays the birds' presence even before you see them.

Grouse and Ptarmigan (family Phasianidae, subfamily Tetraoninae)

are medium-sized birds with moderate to long tails. Adapted to cold, snowy climates, grouse and ptarmigan have feather-covered nostrils and feet. Lateral extensions of the scales on their toes serve as snowshoes in winter. Many species display elaborate courtship behavior.

Blue Grouse   *Dendragapus obscurus*

> **Field marks:** 18". *Male*–uniform gray plumage; **square, black, fan-shaped tail with gray terminal band.** *Female*–brownish plumage.
> **Status:** Widespread and fairly common resident of the coniferous forests through-out the region, including VI; uncommon resident in NCNP; common resident in ONP, MRNP, and CLNP.

The typical grouse of coniferous forests, the blue grouse tolerates human disturbance. In spring, males attract females by hooting. The polygamous males expose a reddish patch of neck skin surrounded by a ring of white feathers. Their eye combs act as barometers of their psychological state—yellow when calm, red when excited or disturbed. Blue grouse nest in open foothills, and the broods follow ripening berry patches up the mountainsides. They winter in Douglas fir thickets just below timberline, sustained by the plentiful supply of needles.

Wild Turkey tom displaying   J. L. WASSINK

Blue Grouse   J. L. WASSINK

Blue Grouse   J. L. WASSINK

Spruce Grouse   *Dendragapus canadensis*

Field marks: 14". *Male*–dark plumage; **red eye comb; black throat and upper breast;** black, fan-shaped tail. *Female*–brown plumage with white markings; short, fan-shaped tail.

Status: Uncommon to rare resident of coniferous forests of the Cascades; more common and widespread in BC east of the Coast Mountains; absent from VI; rare resident in NCNP; accidental in ONP and MRNP; uncommon resident in CLNP.

Even more trusting than blue grouse, spruce grouse often allow humans to approach within feet before flushing. Early settlers are said to have killed these "fool hens" with sticks and stones. Spruce grouse inhabit the vast coniferous forest, preferring lodgepole pine and spruce. Along with strutting, tail-spreading, and short courtship flights, male spruce grouse in this region perform a unique double wing-clap at the end of their display flights.

Ruffed Grouse   *Bonasa umbellus*

Field marks: 17". Brown gray plumage; black neck; **gray fan-shaped tail with black terminal band.**

Status: Fairly common resident in the lower elevations of the region; uncommon resident in NCNP and MRNP; common resident on VI and in ONP; absent from CLNP.

The most widely distributed grouse in the United States, the ruffed grouse prefers deciduous woodlands but also inhabits coniferous forests. This species prefers brushy habitats adjacent to open farmlands or with numerous small openings. Ruffed grouse feed primarily on buds, leaves, and needles. In summer, insects supplement their diet. Males attract females for breeding by "drumming" from a prominent log. The sound, a muffled thumping, is produced by changes in air pressure generated by the beating wings rather than by the wings striking the breast or each other as is sometimes believed.

Sharp-tailed Grouse   *Tympanuchus phasianellus*

Field marks: 18". Brown and buff plumage; **breast and sides marked with dark Vs;** pointed tail.

Status: Remnant local populations along eastern edge of the region; absent from VI and the national parks in this region.

Mainly a prairie grouse, the sharp-tail inhabits some of the more grassy parts of the region. Before dawn on April mornings, the males gather to dance on traditional courting grounds called leks. The dancing establishes a hierarchy among the males and determines which males do the majority of the breeding. Sharp-tails require native grasslands and were once common in those habitats along the eastern edge of the region. As those grasslands disappeared, so did the sharp-tails. Only remnant populations still gather at remaining leks.

Spruce Grouse displaying   L. KAISER

Ruffed Grouse   W. GREEN, VIREO

Sharp-tailed Grouse   J. L. WASSINK

Sage Grouse

Centrocercus urophasianus

Field marks: *Male*–32"; *female*–21". Grayish brown above, blackish below; **long pointed tail.**
Status: Local residents of sagebrush along the eastern edge of the Cascades; absent from BC, VI, and the national parks in this region.

As its name implies, this grouse lives in sagebrush country. Unlike the other members of the order that have tough muscular gizzards to aid in digesting hard seeds and grain, sage grouse have soft membranous gizzards—indicative of their softer diet of the buds and leaves of sagebrush, supplemented with insects during the summer brood-rearing period. Like the sharp-tail, sage grouse gather in spring to display and "boom" on traditional leks. Sixty or more males may gather on a single lek to display. They strut about, wings held low, and stop occasionally to release air from large inflated air sacs on their necks, producing a loud *plop, plop, plop*. Destruction of sagebrush habitat and booming grounds is causing the slow but steady decline of this species.

White-tailed Ptarmigan

Lagopus leucurus

Field marks: 13". Small. *Summer*–mottled brown with **white tail, belly, and wings.** *Winter*–all white except black bill and eyes.
Status: Fairly common resident in the scattered alpine habitats of northern WA, BC, and VI; rare resident in NCNP; uncommon resident in MRNP; absent from ONP and CLNP.

The deliberate and slow-moving white-tailed ptarmigan is the only bird that spends its entire life on the alpine tundra. Its thick coat of feathers protects it from the elements and provides camouflage by matching the colors of the season. In summer, the mottled brown ptarmigan blends with its habitat. As winter approaches, the brown feathers are molted one at a time and replaced by white feathers. By the time snow arrives, the bird is pure white except for its black eyes and beak. In spring the process reverses, with the brown feathers replacing the white ones until the birds once again blend with the summer landscape. Only the tail remains white all year.

The female lays her 6 to 8 buff, faintly spotted eggs in a nest sparsely lined with grass, leaves, and feathers and tucked under a small shrub or by a rock. The chicks hatch and begin searching for insects along the edges of snowfields. They also eat leaves and berries when insects are scarce.

Ptarmigan spend winter days eating the leaves and buds of dwarf willow, the bird's main winter food. Heavily feathered feet and toes act as snowshoes that allow the birds to walk in soft snow. On winter nights, ptarmigan burrow into the snow to escape the bitter cold and biting wind.

Sage Grouse displaying   J. L. WASSINK

White-tailed Ptarmigan in summer plumage
J. L. WASSINK

White-tailed Ptarmigan in fall plumage
J. L. WASSINK

White-tailed Ptarmigan in winter plumage
J. L. WASSINK

Pheasants, Quail, and Partridges (subfamily Phasianinae),

like the rest of the Phasianidae family, scratch the surface of the ground for seeds and insects. In contrast to grouse, pheasants, quail, and partridges have nostrils and tarsi that are bare of feathers and have spurs on their lower legs for fighting. Hunters have transplanted these upland game birds into many habitats they would not otherwise inhabit. Of the birds featured here, only the California quail and the mountain quail are native to this region, and even they have been introduced into new areas. The northern bobwhite is native to the southeastern United States, and the ring-necked pheasant, the chukar, and the gray partridge were introduced from the Far East.

California Quail   *Callipepla californica*

Field marks: 10". *Male*–bold black and white pattern on the head with buffy forehead; **black, curved head plume;** gray blue back; chestnut sides with white slash marks. *Female*–gray and white pattern on the head; **small head plume;** gray blue back; scaly belly.
Status: Resident in suitable habitats at lower elevations throughout the Cascades but more common in the southern part of the region; absent from the Coast Mountains; introduced and now common resident on VI; rare resident in NCNP; common resident in ONP; accidental in MRNP; absent from CLNP.

The most widespread quail in this region, the California quail inhabits virtually all open brushy habitats and agricultural lands. In fall, these gregarious birds gather in large coveys consisting of several family groups. A sentinel commonly perches in a nearby tree while the covey feeds. At dusk, California quail gather and roost in trees. If alarmed, the birds flush separately, each flying in a different direction than the others. After landing, the scattered covey regroups to an assembly call, *key-CAR-go*.

Mountain Quail   *Oreortyx pictus*

Field marks: 11". Gray head, back, and breast; chestnut throat; **long, straight head plume;** chestnut flanks with white bars.
Status: Fairly common resident in suitable habitat along the western and southern edges of the Cascades; also found on eastern slopes north to about the WA border; absent from the Coast Mountains, NCNP, and MRNP; rare local resident on extreme southern VI and in ONP and CLNP.

Mountain quail inhabit dry, open areas of early successional stages of timberland—the brushy habitats resulting from burns and logging. Even where they are relatively plentiful, their fondness for cover makes them difficult to observe. Mountain quail rarely flush when disturbed. Instead, they escape by running to dense cover. Unlike California quail, mountain quail roost on the ground or in low bushes.

California Quail J. HOFFMAN, VIREO

Mountain Quail J. D. CUNNINGHAM, VISUALS UNLIMITED

Ring-necked Pheasant
Phasianus colchicus

Field marks: 33". *Male*–large; **multicolored plumage;** long tapered tail. *Female*–mottled brown plumage.

Status: Introduced; common resident near agricultural areas in extreme southern BC, VI, and the Cascades; rare resident in NCNP; accidental in MRNP; absent from ONP and CLNP.

Originally introduced into the United States near Albany, Oregon, by Judge Owen Denny, the ring-necked pheasant is highly prized by hunters, who have introduced them into virtually all available habitats across the nation. Closely linked to agriculture, ring-necked pheasants feed on weed seeds, insects, and waste grain. They nest in weedy margins and alfalfa fields, where they are sometimes killed by mowing machines and combines. With "cleaner" farming eliminating those weedy margins, ring-necked pheasant populations have begun to decline. The polygamous male attracts hens in spring by beating his wings and crowing from a favored location within his home range. They spend summers alone or in family groups, but commonly form large flocks in late winter.

Chukar
Alectoris chukar

Field marks: 13". Gray back; **barred black-and-white flanks; white face and throat outlined with black; red legs.**

Status: Introduced; local resident in arid country; absent from VI and the region's national parks.

Introduced from the foothills of the Himalayas, chukars find the arid country near steep rocky slopes of this region much to their liking. They thrive in climates where summers are short and hot and winters only moderately cold and long. Snow forces chukars from the higher slopes to lower valleys. Persistently deep snow may cause heavy losses. Chukars seek bunchgrass and sagebrush habitats during the spring nesting season. From midmorning to afternoon, chukars forage for the seeds of cheatgrass, Russian thistle, and other weeds. During the heat of summer, these birds make daily trips to water before roosting in brushy draws.

Gray Partridge
Perdix perdix

Field marks: 12". **Orange brown face;** gray back and breast; brown belly. *In flight*–**rusty tail.**

Status: Introduced; fairly common in irrigated farmlands along the eastern edge of the region; less common in the west; not found on VI or in any of the national parks.

Found in coveys all year except during the nesting season, these vocal birds can be heard in all seasons. Because they prefer dense cover, gray partridges are seldom seen except during the fall and winter when snow covers their hiding places, forcing them to congregate along roads and in open farm fields. When disturbed, the entire covey flushes at once in a noisy explosion of beating wings and hoarse calls. The covey stays together in flight, then drops out of sight on a nearby knoll or ridge. The birds roost in a circle on the ground, like bobwhite, or plunge into a soft snowdrift to spend cold winter nights.

Ring-necked Pheasant rooster   J. L. WASSINK

Chukar   T. J. ULRICH

Gray Partridge   A. G. NELSON

CRANES, RAILS, AND COOTS (order Gruiformes) are a small
but diverse group of wading birds. All have long legs. Other features, including body size
and shape, bill size, and neck length, vary considerably.

Cranes (family Gruidae) are tall, long-legged birds with long necks and heavy
bodies. Cranes fly with their heads extended, distinguishing them from the herons. They
lay two eggs per year.

Sandhill Crane   *Grus canadensis*

Field marks: 48". **Gray plumage; red crown.** *In flight–***fly with neck
outstretched.**
Status: Local summer resident east of the Cascade and Coast range crests; mainly
migrant in the west; local breeder in southern BC and on VI; accidental in NCNP;
rare winter visitor in ONP; absent from MRNP and CLNP.

Stately but shy, sandhill cranes mate for life and, just prior to nesting in spring,
perform a balletlike dance to reinforce the pair bond. In synchronized movement,
the cranes dip, bow, leap, stretch, and call to each other. As they dance, the birds
use their bills to toss sticks and grass. Sandhills nest in shallow, wet meadows. They
forage in nearby meadows for small insects, amphibians, rodents, grain, seeds, and
roots but invariably return to water to roost for the night. The reddish brown
young birds mature sexually and display the slate gray plumage of the adult when
they are 2 years old. Sandhill cranes migrate to and from their wintering grounds
in California, the Southwest, and Mexico in large flocks, stopping at many favored
resting spots east of the Cascades. In the west, they may stop in the Willamette
Valley or along the Columbia River. Pitt-Addington Wildlife Management Area,
along the Pitt River, is one of the few places in the lower mainland of Canada
where you can observe sandhill cranes.

Rails (family Rallidae) are small to medium-sized birds that inhabit the emergent
vegetation of marshes and lake shores. Their compact bodies, short necks, long legs, and
long toes enable them to move easily through the reeds in pursuit of small invertebrates
and insects. Shy and retiring, they are more often heard than seen. Rails build their nests
just above the surface of the water and have large clutches. The adults share the
domestic duties.

Virginia Rail   *Rallus limicola*

Field marks: 9". **Long bill;** gray cheeks; **rusty breast;** barred flanks.
Status: Fairly common to rare breeding summer resident in habitats throughout
the Cascades, on VI, and in ONP; absent from NCNP, MRNP, and CLNP.

In spring, sounds like that of iron being pounded on an anvil ring resound through
the marsh. Sharp-eared birders and female Virginia rails note the presence of an
amorous male Virginia rail. Almost immediately after hatching, the chicks are
ready to run, swim, and dive, and quickly learn to capture the snails, slugs,
earthworms, and insects that make up their diet. When flushed, Virginia rails
launch into a short, fluttery flight with legs dangling.

Sandhill Crane   J. L. WASSINK

Sandhill Crane family   J. L. WASSINK

Virginia Rail   F. K. SCHLEICHER, VIREO

Sora

Porzana carolina

Field marks: 9". Stocky; **yellow chickenlike bill; black face and bib;** short wings; long yellowish green legs.

Status: Fairly common summer resident in the lower elevations of the region; rare breeding summer resident on VI and in NCNP and ONP; absent from MRNP and CLNP.

Noisy like Virginia rails, soras betray their presence with a variety of sounds from quiet peeping to loud whinnying. Still, knowing soras are present makes them no easier to see because they spend most of their time in extensive stands of dense emergent vegetation. There, soras search for insects, their heads down and their tails up and twitching almost constantly. Light enough to walk over floating water plants, they swim only when necessary. Soras place their nests in tussocks or suspend them just above the water. They lay and incubate up to 18 eggs by arranging them in two layers and rotating them regularly. The downy young are black and accompany their parents on feeding forays soon after hatching.

American Coot

Fulica americana

Field marks: 14". **Slate gray plumage;** white bill; **white under tail;** head rocks forward and backward while swimming.

Status: Common breeding summer resident throughout the lower elevations of this region, including on southern VI and in ONP; rare migrant in NCNP; absent from MRNP and CLNP.

Look for American coots on ponds or marshes with open water and in dense stands of cattails or reeds. Highly territorial, "mud hens" sometimes battle over nesting space. Unlike other rails, coots have lobed toes, which aid them while swimming—something they do much more than other rails. Coots have their own peculiar way of swimming, with their heads bobbing back and forth. When flushed, they flail the surface of the water for long distances before finally becoming airborne, legs dangling. Coots eat seeds, leaves, roots, insects, snails, worms, and small fish. They can dive to more than 25 feet to feed on plants. They also tip in shallow water like the puddle ducks and graze on shore. Coots are not above waiting on the surface to steal plants from feeding canvasbacks or other diving ducks. American coots from this region winter along the Pacific coast from Bella Coola, British Columbia, to southern California.

Sora   J. L. WASSINK

American Coot   J. L. WASSINK

American Coot territorial display   J. L. WASSINK

SHOREBIRDS, GULLS, AND TERNS (order

Charadriiformes) are small to medium-sized birds, most of whom, as their name implies, patrol the shorelines of lakes, ponds, rivers, and marshes for aquatic insects and other small invertebrates. While most have long legs for feeding in up to several inches of water without getting wet, some have webbed feet that enable them to feed while swimming. A few prefer uplands to the water's edge. Long, pointed wings facilitate their migratory lifestyle. This group includes the arctic tern, one of the world's greatest travelers—it nests in the Arctic and migrates to the Antarctic. Plovers and sandpipers, also members of this order, nest in Canada and Alaska and fly as far south as Central America to winter. The sexes are similarly outfitted in cryptic shades of white, gray, and brown.

Plovers (family Charadriidae) are small to medium-sized shorebirds with rela-

tively short bills, distinctly marked heads, and shorter necks than other shorebirds. Their long, pointed wings bear highly visible white stripes. Plovers run in spurts, holding their bodies horizontal. Plovers nest directly on the ground and usually lay 4 eggs.

Semipalmated Plover   *Charadrius semipalmatus*

Field marks: 7". **Stubby orange bill with black tip;** distinctively marked head with white forehead, black stripe in front of and below the eyes, and gray brown crown; **single, narrow, black breast band**; gray brown back and wings; orange legs.
Status: Fairly common migrant at lower elevations along the west side of the region, on VI, and in ONP; absent from NCNP, MRNP, and CLNP.

In spring and fall, large flocks of semipalmated plovers traverse the region as they travel between their wintering areas along the southern Pacific coast and their nesting grounds in Alaska and northern Canada. While en route, they can be seen resting and feeding on freshly plowed fields as well as area beaches and mudflats. These plovers rarely wade in the water, preferring instead to race about on still-damp sand or flats, where they pick bits of food off the surface.

Killdeer   *Charadrius vociferus*

Field marks: 10". Brown back; white underneath; **double breast band;** rusty tail.
Status: Widespread breeding summer resident throughout this area; unusual breeding summer resident in NCNP; common breeding summer resident on VI and in ONP; rare summer resident in MRNP and CLNP.

Nesting killdeer occupy a wide variety of open habitats: shorelines, pastures, golf courses, roadsides, and lawns. They lay their eggs directly on bare ground. Before and after nesting, killdeer frequent shorelines more than while nesting. Unlike some birds that sit tight on the nest almost until they are stepped on, the killdeer slips off her nest while the intruder approaches. If the intruder wanders too close to the nest or the young, the adult feigns a broken wing to draw the danger away from the nest. Killdeer feed mainly on insects they pick from the surface of the ground.

Semipalmated Plover   T. J. ULRICH

Killdeer   J. L. WASSINK

Killdeer nesting   J. L. WASSINK

Stilts and Avocets (family Recurvirostridae) are medium to large

shorebirds whose Latin name describes their long, thin, upturned or straight bills. As their exceptionally long legs suggest, they feed on insects and small aquatic invertebrates in deeper water than most other shorebirds do.

American Avocet — *Recurvirostra americana*

Field marks: 18". **Light brown head, neck, and breast;** black wings with white bars; white below; **long, black, upturned bill;** long, thin, blue gray legs; webbed toes.

Status: Fairly common summer resident in the lower elevations along the eastern edge of the region; rare migrant on VI and in ONP; absent from NCNP, MRNP, and CLNP.

One of the most striking shorebirds, the American avocet inhabits alkaline ponds of arid mountain basins. It frequents the shallows, where it feeds on aquatic insects and other invertebrates by sweeping its bill from side to side. The sweeping action stirs the bottom mud, exposing small aquatic animals and insects, which the bird promptly eats. Avocets nest on expansive flats, shorelines, or islands with little or no vegetation. The female lays 3 or 4 olive, blotched eggs either in a shallow depression in the sand or on a small platform of grass near the water. Soon after hatching, the young leave the nest and follow the adults to the water. If the family is disturbed, the young scurry for cover while the adults use the broken-wing ploy to distract the intruder. Avocets swim readily. Their call is a loud *wheet, wheet.*

Sandpipers (family Scolopacidae) are a large and diverse group of wading and

upland birds clothed in dull gray, buff, or brown plumage and identifiable by variations in wing, rump, or tail markings. Their legs and bills are long and slender, ideal for probing soft muck or shallow water for small invertebrates. Except for the phalaropes, the sexes are virtually identical. Sandpipers breed on the barren grounds and muskeg of the Arctic and subarctic and winter in South America.

Long-billed Curlew — *Numenius americanus*

Field marks: 24". Brown plumage; large; **long, decurved bill;** cinnamon wing linings.

Status: Uncommon migrant and local summer resident along the eastern edge of the region; rare winter visitor on VI and in ONP; absent from the other national parks in this region.

Long-billed curlews nest in scattered colonies in the remaining grasslands along the eastern slope of the Cascade and Coast ranges, often far from water. The nests consist of slight hollows in the ground lined with forbs and grasses. The sexes share incubation duties for the 4 eggs. While raising their young on the grasslands, curlews feed mostly on insects. Other times of the year, they frequent tidal flats and beaches and use their long bills like forceps to extract shellfish and various other invertebrates from well below the ground. Call is a drawn out *cur-lee-e-e.*

American Avocet   J. L. WASSINK

Long-billed Curlew   A. G. NELSON

Marbled Godwit

Limosa fedoa

Field marks: 18". Size and color of curlew but with cinnamon wing linings; **long orange upturned bill with a black tip.**

Status: Uncommon migrant along the southern and eastern edges of the region; rare winter visitor on VI and in ONP; absent from the other national parks in this region.

Second in size only to the long-billed curlew, marbled godwits breed in northern Montana, North Dakota, and south-central Canada. The female seeks out a grassy hollow on the plains in which to lay her eggs. The marbled godwits that pass through this region winter along the coast of California, where, like most shorebirds, they live on a diet of insects, worms, mollusks, and crustaceans. Birders will easily recognize this bird by its call because it calls its own name: *god-wit*. Marbled godwits commonly gather in small flocks and feed by rapidly thrusting their bills into soft mudflats.

Spotted Sandpiper

Actitis macularia

Field marks: 8". Brown above, **spotted white below;** body usually tilted forward; **teeters up and down almost constantly;** flies with rapid wing beats on down-curved wings.

Status: Fairly common summer resident throughout the region; unusual breeding summer resident in NCNP and MRNP; uncommon breeding summer resident on VI and in ONP; locally common summer visitor in CLNP.

Watch for the spotted sandpiper as it runs and teeters along rocky or gravelly shorelines of rivers and streams. A solitary bird that does not flock like the other sandpipers, it is the only small sandpiper that nests throughout the central and northern United States. When disturbed, it flies out over the water on short, stiff wing beats and alights a short distance down the shore—all the time calling *wheet-wheet-wheet*. Instead of probing like other sandpipers, the spotted sandpiper catches insects and other invertebrates on the surface.

Solitary Sandpiper

Tringa solitaria

Field marks: 8". Short, olive bill; **white eye ring;** gray or olive brown speckled above; streaked breast; barred tail; **long, dark legs.** *In flight*–plain dark wings.

Status: Rare migrant throughout the region; rare migrant on VI and in NCNP, ONP, and MRNP; absent from CLNP.

Although found along the same streams, lakes, and marshes as the spotted sandpiper during migration, the solitary sandpiper is usually seen alone. Its flight is buoyant and swallowlike. After landing, this sandpiper typically keeps its wings raised for a second or two. While on the ground, it bobs its tail. Solitary sandpipers that pass through this area breed in Alaska or north-central Canada and winter along the Pacific coast of Mexico.

Marbled Godwit   J. L. WASSINK

Spotted Sandpiper   J. L. WASSINK

Solitary Sandpiper   J. DUNNING, VIREO

Greater Yellowlegs

Tringa melanoleuca

Field marks: 14". Mottled grayish brown upperparts; **long, slim, slightly upturned bill;** lightly streaked or barred breast and belly; **long yellow legs; 3- to 5-note whistle.**

Status: Occasional to common migrant throughout the region, rare at upper elevations; rare migrant and winter visitor in NCNP and MRNP; common migrant on VI and in ONP; absent from CLNP.

Greater yellowlegs nest on the tundra and muskeg of north-central Canada and Alaska and winter along the California and the Gulf coasts. While migrating through the Pacific mountains, they stop to rest and feed in shallow waters bordered by mudflats. They rush about in the shallow water, catching small fish and aquatic invertebrates with rapid sweeps of their bills or by pecking food from the surface. They are usually seen alone or with loose groups of fewer than 10 birds. Greater yellowlegs take flight readily when disturbed and fly with their long legs extended well beyond their tails.

Lesser Yellowlegs

Tringa flavipes

Field marks: 10". Plain gray brown plumage; **bright yellow legs;** long, slim bill; **1- to 3-note whistle.**

Status: Rare to occasional migrant throughout the region and on VI, rare at upper elevations; rare migrant and winter visitor in NCNP and ONP; absent from MRNP or CLNP.

Watch for the lesser yellowlegs probing in the mud along the edges of marshes and slow rivers during spring migration. Lesser yellowlegs also feed by skimming invertebrates from the surface of the water or the ground. This bird does not feed by sweeping its bill as the greater yellowlegs does. Smaller, tamer, and quieter than its larger look-alike, the lesser yellowlegs often bobs its head before taking flight. More gregarious than the greater yellowlegs, these birds often form flocks of from several dozen to several hundred birds.

Least Sandpiper

Calidris minutilla

Field marks: 6". **Sparrow size; ruddy colored above;** short, slightly drooped, black bill; olive yellow legs and feet.

Status: Common migrant in the lower elevations throughout the region, on VI, and in ONP; absent from the other national parks in this region.

The least sandpiper, the smallest North American shorebird, breeds on the coastal tundra of northern Canada and winters along the Pacific, Atlantic, and Gulf coasts. Least sandpipers pass through the Pacific mountains in spring and fall in the company of other shorebirds. They frequent mudflats and marsh edges throughout the year, feeding in the drier mud and sand well away from the edge of the water. Least sandpipers feed either by probing in the mud or by picking food from the surface. Migrating flocks take flight as single units, zigging and zagging in unison.

Greater Yellowlegs   J. L. WASSINK

Lesser Yellowlegs   J. L. WASSINK

Least Sandpiper   T. J. ULRICH

Long-billed Dowitcher
Limnodromus scolopaceus

Field marks: 12". Plump profile; long, black bill; reddish below; barred flanks. *In flight*–**white rump and lower back; distinctive *keek* call.**
Status: Occasional to abundant migrant at lower elevations of the region, on VI, and in ONP; absent from the region's other national parks.

Long-billed dowitchers breed on northern coast of Alaska and winter on the Pacific, Atlantic, and Gulf coasts, passing through the Pacific mountains in April and October. Small flocks of these birds gather in open, grassy marshes, either feeding by probing in belly-deep water or resting on mudflats. Unlike most shorebirds, long-billed dowitchers often dunk their heads underwater while searching for insect larvae, tiny snails, and seeds.

Common Snipe
Gallinago gallinago

Field marks: 11". **Extremely long bill; stocky body;** short legs; brown plumage.
Status: Common summer resident throughout the lower elevations of the region; rare at higher elevations; rare breeding summer resident in NCNP; fairly common breeding summer resident on VI and ONP; accidental in MRNP; rare summer resident in CLNP.

Look for the common snipe perched on a roadside fence post near soggy meadows. Its extremely long bill makes it easy to recognize. Like other shorebirds, the snipe uses its bill to probe for invertebrates in moist ground. When the sensitive tip encounters food, the bird uses the bill's prehensile tip to quickly grasp the morsel and pull it to the surface. Snipes nest in boggy areas, often near beaver ponds, on small hummocks hidden in the tall grass. The male snipe establishes his territory with winnowing flight—sudden, deep dives that produce a wavering sound as air rushes through the bird's outer tail feathers. When threatened, the snipe relies on its protective coloring for security, flushing only at the last instant and soon dropping back into tall vegetation.

Wilson's Phalarope
Phalaropus tricolor

Field marks: 9". *Male*–brown plumage; white below; **dark stripe through the eye and down the neck;** long thin bill. *Female*–similar to the male but with **bright chestnut markings on sides of neck and on back.**
Status: Common migrant and summer resident east of the Cascade and Coast range crests; uncommon in the western parts of this region; rare migrant and summer resident on VI and in NCNP; rare migrant in ONP; vagrant in MRNP; absent from CLNP.

In this species, the females are more colorful than the males—and the role reversal extends beyond the plumage. The females establish the territories, court the males, and, after laying the eggs, leave the small clutch for the male to incubate. Phalaropes feed both in the hunt-and-peck manner of other shorebirds and in their own unique way: whirling in circles on the surface of shallow water. The spinning action creates a vortex that stirs the bottom muck and sucks it to the surface, where the phalarope picks out the food without even wetting its head.

Long-billed Dowitcher T. J. ULRICH

Common Snipe J. L. WASSINK

Male Wilson's Phalarope and Female Wilson's Phalarope (*inset*) J. L. WASSINK

Gulls and Terns (family Laridae) have webbed feet and long, pointed wings. They are graceful and adept in flight.

Gulls (subfamily Larinae) have heavy bills that hook at the tip, a feature that enables them to eat almost anything. Unlike terns, gulls often float on the water. Gulls traditionally fed on dead or dying fish or patrolled the shorelines for grasshoppers and crickets, but they soon learned to take advantage of easy food provided by humans. Look for gulls in freshly plowed or flooded fields, city parks, landfills, or even supermarket parking lots. They also sometimes prey on the eggs and young of other birds. The sexes appear similar. Gulls lay 2 to 5 eggs. The young of some species take several years to mature and gain adult plumage. Gulls are long-lived; many banding records document birds over 20 years old.

California Gull   *Larus californicus*

Field marks: White plumage, dark mantle; **yellow green legs and feet; yellow bill with red and black spots** near the tip of the lower mandible.
Status: Common migrant throughout the region and on VI; locally common breeding summer resident, especially east of the Cascades and along the Columbia River; rare resident in NCNP and ONP; rare summer visitor in MRNP; locally common summer resident in CLNP.

Like ring-billed gulls, California gulls nest in colonies on sparsely vegetated islands. These opportunistic feeders flock anywhere food is abundant, including city parks and supermarket parking lots. In 1848, these birds descended on the swarms of crickets that were devouring the crops of the Mormon settlers in the Salt Lake Valley, and saved the crops. In return, Utah designated the California gull as the state bird. It winters along the Pacific coast of extreme southern British Columbia, Washington, Oregon, and California.

California Gull

California Gull in flight

Glaucous-winged Gull

Larus glaucescens

Field marks: 23". Yellow bill with red spot; white head; pale gray back; pale gray wings with **pale gray wing tips;** pink legs.

Status: Locally abundant migrant and breeding resident along the western edge of the region and on VI; rare migrant and summer resident in NCNP; abundant breeding resident in ONP; absent from MRNP and CLNP.

A bird of the Pacific coastline, glaucous-winged gulls nest from northern Washington to Alaska. They interbreed with herring gulls in Alaska and with western gulls in this region. The hybrids display plumage characteristics of both species. Although primarily scavengers, glaucous-winged gulls also feed on mollusks, which they drop from midair to crack them on the rocks below. In winter, these gulls disperse as far south as Baja California and east toward the Cascade and Coast ranges, mostly along river valleys such as the lower Skeena River in British Columbia and the Columbia River in Washington.

Ring-billed Gull

Larus delawarensis

Field marks: 19". White plumage; gray wings; **black ring around bill; yellowish legs and feet.**

Status: Common migrant throughout the region; local breeding resident south from central WA; local winter resident mainly west of the Cascades; rare in the Coast Mountains; uncommon on VI; uncommon resident in NCNP; uncommon breeding resident in ONP; vagrant in MRNP; rare summer visitor in CLNP.

Like most other gulls, ring-billed gulls nest in colonies, usually on islands with little or low vegetation. These opportunistic feeders follow the farmer's plow for overturned tidbits, frequent garbage dumps, and flock to newly mown fields to eat insects. The most common gull in the region, ring-billed gulls have adapted and expanded their range, moving into residential areas even though their traditional habitat has shrunk.

Glaucous-winged Gull

Ring-billed Gull

Juvenile Ring-billed Gull

Terns (subfamily Sterninae), unlike the heavy-bodied gulls, have thin, pointed bills, narrow wings, and forked tails—features that make them look delicate and graceful. They fly lightly over the water in search of small fish, plunging in a headfirst dive to capture their prey. Terns seldom alight on the water, preferring instead to rest on shore or on floating debris. They lay 2 or 3 eggs per clutch.

Caspian Tern   *Sterna caspia*

Field marks: 21". Large; **large head;** heavy red bill; **crested black cap;** short, slightly forked tail.
Status: Regular migrant and local summer resident mostly throughout OR and northern CA; fairly common migrant on VI; vagrant in NCNP; abundant breeding bird in ONP; absent from MRNP and CLNP.

The largest tern in North America, the Caspian tern most often nests on gravel islands or beaches. Although it nests in large colonies elsewhere, in Oregon and northern California it tends to limit itself to 1 or 2 pairs in a colony with another species. This solitary bird is the least sociable of the terns and is less graceful than the smaller terns. The Caspian tern acts like a gull at times—alighting on the water, pirating food, and preying on the eggs and young of other birds.

Forster's Tern   *Sterna forsteri*

Field marks: 15". Pale gray above, white below; **black crown and nape;** orangish bill; **tail has white outer edges.**
Status: Fairly common migrant and local summer resident east of the Cascade crest; occasional west of the mountains; rare summer visitor on VI and in ONP; absent from NCNP, MRNP, and CLNP.

Forster's terns are the most common black-capped tern in the region. They prefer the Great Basin side of the mountains, where they frequent shallow marshes with emergent vegetation and islands for nesting. Forster's terns forage over open water, where they dive for fish, pick bits of food from the water's surface, or take insects out of the air. After a summer of raising their young, they move south and west to the Pacific coast from California to South America.

Black Tern   *Chlidonias niger*

Field marks: 10". **All black plumage;** gray wings.
Status: Migrant and local summer resident east of the Cascade and Coast range crests; rare migrant on west side, on VI, and in ONP; absent from the region's other national parks.

Tame and almost friendly birds, black terns prefer marshes with abundant emergent vegetation. Nests are a shallow cup of reeds on a muskrat house or a low tussock or a frail platform among the reeds. More insectivorous than the other terns, black terns hawk insects from the air or skim them from the surface of the water.

Caspian Tern   T. J. ULRICH

Forster's Tern   J. L. WASSINK

Black Tern   D. & M. ZIMMERMAN, VIREO

PIGEONS AND DOVES (order Columbiformes, family Columbidae)
are ground-feeding birds with small heads, short legs, long pointed wings, and fan-shaped or pointed tails. They bob their heads and coo when they walk. Pigeons and doves eat seeds, grains, nuts, and berries and need a plentiful supply of water daily to help soften the dry hard seeds they eat. Unlike most birds, they swallow without raising their heads. Their nests are flimsy, loosely constructed arrangements of sticks. Doves and pigeons lay 1 or 2 eggs (but may raise up to four broods each year) and share the incubation. The female incubates during the day, the male at night. Pigeons and doves feed their young, or squabs, "pigeon milk"—a curdy mixture of skin sloughed in the crop and partially digested seeds.

Band-tailed Pigeon   *Columba fasciata*

Field marks: 15". Slate blue plumage; broad, **pale terminal tail band; white crescent on nape;** yellow, black-tipped bill.
Status: Fairly common summer resident throughout the region and on VI; uncommon breeding summer resident in NCNP and ONP; common migrant and summer resident in MRNP; rare migrant and summer resident in CLNP.

The largest pigeons in North America, band-tailed pigeons are common in open conifer stands, where they seek out large Douglas fir trees to hold their flimsy nests. Territorial displays include a *rook-a-roo* call. Gregarious and somewhat nomadic, except while raising their single squab, they wander about in small flocks searching for plentiful supplies of acorns, wild fruits, and berries. Birds from the Pacific mountains winter primarily in central California.

Rock Dove   *Columba livia*

Field marks: 13". Large stout body; **white rump;** plumage color varies widely.
Status: Common resident throughout the region and on VI, less common at higher elevations; absent from NCNP and MRNP; rare in ONP and CLNP.

The wild form of the domestic pigeon, the rock dove immigrated from the Old World. Selective breeding of domestic stock has produced diverse plumages: black, brown, white, and various combinations of these colors. Rock doves may raise several broods each year. They usually nest in buildings or other human-made structures but also use cliffs and crevices.

Mourning Dove   *Zenaida macroura*

Field marks: 12". Small; grayish brown plumage; **long, pointed tail; wings whistle in flight.**
Status: Regular migrant and summer resident throughout the region; rare migrant and breeding summer resident on VI and in NCNP; fairly common breeding summer resident in ONP; vagrant in MRNP; unusual migrant and summer resident in CLNP.

The mourning dove lives and breeds in virtually all habitats in the region, making it a familiar sight to almost everyone. It builds its nest, a haphazard pile of sticks, either on the ground or in a tree, where a strong wind may easily destroy it. During the breeding season, the male has a small iridescent spot on his neck, and his blue eye ring and red legs intensify in color. Most mourning doves move south in fall, but some winter here.

Band-tailed Pigeon   D. & M. ZIMMERMAN, VIREO

Rock Dove   J. L. WASSINK

Mourning Dove   J. L. WASSINK

OWLS (order Strigiformes) are one of the most easily recognized groups of birds.

These birds of the night are equipped with large eyes set forward on their heads to provide binocular vision, which is invaluable in locating and focusing on fast-moving prey. Extremely sensitive ears, unequal in size and located behind facial disks that apparently help focus the sound, pinpoint prey in total darkness. Flight feathers, with their soft leading edges, allow almost silent flight. Owls swallow small prey whole but tear larger prey into bite-sized pieces with their powerful talons and strong hooked beaks. They regurgitate the indigestible bones, fur, and feathers as pellets. The females are generally larger than the males and begin incubating their eggs immediately after laying the first egg, allowing the young to hatch at intervals. The oldest, and therefore the largest, chick insists on being fed first. Only when it is satiated does the next one get to eat. In lean years, the youngest and weakest may die, but this method maximizes the chance that at least some of the young will survive. Each species of owl has a distinctive call.

Western Screech-owl   *Otus kennicottii*

Field marks: 9". Small; **yellow eyes; ear tufts;** grayish plumage. *Voice*–a quavering whistle.
Status: Fairly common resident throughout the region, on VI, and in NCNP and ONP; uncommon resident in MRNP; rare resident in CLNP.

The western screech-owl occupies many habitats in the Pacific mountains: suburbs, orchards, farms, river bottoms, aspens, and ponderosa pine forests. They take mice from meadows and large insects from the air or from foliage, as well as catching and eating bats, crayfish, fish, reptiles, frogs, worms, and birds wherever they find them. Screech-owls nest in tree cavities, laying 4 or 5 eggs in early spring. The adults are fearless, sometimes attacking trespassers who venture too near the nest.

Great Horned Owl   *Bubo virginianus*

Field marks: 22". Large; **ear tufts;** horizontal bars on belly. *Voice*–a deep, low *hoo-hoo-hoooo hoo-hoo*.
Status: Common resident throughout the region; uncommon resident on VI; unusual resident in NCNP and MRNP; common resident in ONP and CLNP.

The great horned owl is the most common owl in all types of woodlands. This highly efficient predator prefers rabbits but takes a wide variety of birds, mammals, and reptiles. Remains of dogs, cats, skunks, rattlesnakes, and even peregrine falcons have been found in their castings. When the February breeding season rolls around, the owls take possession of an old hawk or heron nest, a tree hollow, an appropriate ledge or crevice, or even an undisturbed corner in a building and lay 2 to 4 eggs. Like screech-owls, great horned owls fearlessly defend their young.

Fledgling Screech-owl   J. L. WASSINK

Screech-owl   J. L. WASSINK

Fledgling Great Horned Owl
                    J. L. WASSINK

Great Horned Owl
J. L. WASSINK

Long-eared Owl
Asio otus

Field marks: 15". Medium size; **long ear tufts;** rusty face; smaller, slimmer than great horned owl; **vertical barring on belly.** *Voice*–one or more long *hoo*s.
Status: Uncommon resident throughout much of the region; more common east of the crest; vagrant in NCNP; rare winter visitor on VI and in ONP; rare summer visitor in MRNP; absent from CLNP.

Like the great horned owl, the long-eared owl inhabits a wide variety of habitats, although it seems to prefer dense forests or streamside timber. The highly nocturnal long-eared owl hunts small mammals, mostly mice, at night, then finds an inconspicuous spot close to the trunk of a shady tree to roost during the day. Like many other owls, it remodels an old crow, hawk, heron, or magpie nest to suit its needs and lays from 3 to 7 white eggs. The long-eared owl's buoyant and erratic flight is easy to recognize.

Short-eared Owl
Asio flammeus

Field marks: 15". Medium size; appears "earless"; **light belly with vertical stripes.** *In flight*–black "wrist" marks; **flies with a buoyant lilt.** *Voice*–a raspy bark.
Status: Uncommon resident in open habitats throughout the region; vagrant in NCNP; rare winter visitor on VI and in ONP; absent from MRNP and CLNP.

Powered by slow, relaxed wing strokes, the short-eared owl flies with a characteristic erratic bounce. A diurnal bird of open country, this owl commonly perches on fence posts or drifts low over the grasslands, searching for small rodents in broad daylight where it is easily seen. Since it inhabits areas without trees, the short-eared owl sleeps and nests on the ground. A slight depression lined with a few grasses or feathers holds the 4 to 9 white eggs that the female incubates almost exclusively.

Barn Owl
Tyto alba

Field marks: 14". Large, white, **heart-shaped facial disk;** dark eyes; light golden brown above with small black spots, white below with small black spots; long legs.
Status: Casual to rare resident in open country throughout the Cascades, more common west of the crest; absent from the Coast Mountains; rare resident on VI and in NCNP; absent from ONP; vagrant in MRNP; rare summer visitor in CLNP.

After a night of quartering low over open fields, barn owls return to roost in a secluded corner of a barn, silo, church steeple or another building, a tree cavity, a small cave, or a crevice on a small cliff or ravine wall. They do not build a nest but simply lay their 3 to 11 pure white eggs on whatever is there, usually their castings. When approached at its nest, a barn owl will lower its head and move it from side to side. Premier mousers, barn owls have demonstrated their ability to catch mice in darkness, using their ears to pinpoint their prey and guide their sharp talons in for the kill.

Long-eared Owl T. J. ULRICH

Short-eared Owl J. L. WASSINK

Short-eared Owl showing "ears"
J. L. WASSINK

Barn Owl C. D. MARTI, VIREO

Snowy Owl
Nyctea scandiaca

Field marks: 24". Yellow eyes; no ear tufts; **white plumage** with small black spots or bars.
Status: Rare winter visitor to the region; not found in NCNP or CLNP; uncommon winter visitor on VI and in ONP; vagrant in MRNP.

Snowy owls nest and raise their young on the open tundra of northern Alaska and northern Canada. After completing that task, most snowy owls stay there, passing the harsh winters by hunting during the day and roosting at night. In some years, prompted by a short supply of rodents, they move south, wandering into southern British Columbia and northern Washington, where they attract the attention of birders.

Spotted Owl
Strix occidentalis

Field marks: 18". Medium size; round head; no ear tufts; dark eyes; dark brown above with white spots, **tan below with dark horizontal bars.**
Status: Rare to unusual resident primarily at upper elevations of the Cascades; absent from VI and the Coast Mountains; unusual resident in NCNP; fairly common breeding resident in ONP; rare resident in MRNP and CLNP.

Living only in dense, old-growth spruce and fir forests of the Cascade and Pacific coast ranges of southern British Columbia, Washington, Oregon, and California, the spotted owl is a candidate for the United States Endangered Species List. National efforts to protect the owl's habitat from logging has caused much controversy. Spotted owls lay 2 or 3 eggs in nests in a tree cavities or in abandoned hawk or raven nests. Each pair of spotted owls requires several hundred acres of territory to successfully raise their young. They feed primarily on small rodents.

Great Gray Owl
Strix nebulosa

Field marks: 28". Large; large head; **no ear tufts; concentric circles in facial disks;** yellow eyes; **white "bow tie."** *Voice*–a series of deep, booming *hoos*.
Status: Rare resident of montane forests throughout the region; casual on VI; vagrant in NCNP; absent from ONP and MRNP; rare resident in CLNP.

An inhabitant of open meadows and forest clearings near mature stands of conifers, the great gray owl hunts from an elevated perch. It takes hares, pine squirrels, mice, and small birds, but its main prey is pocket gophers. Although seldom seen, the great gray owl is almost indifferent to people. It claims an old hawk or crow nest to contain its 2 to 5 eggs, which it lays when snow is still on the ground. Less nocturnal than some of the other owls, the great gray often hunts at dawn and dusk. This owl of the north sports a thick coat of feathers that makes it look larger than it is.

Snowy Owl   J. L. WASSINK

Spotted Owl   A. & S. CAREY, VIREO

Great Gray Owl   J. L. WASSINK

Northern Pygmy-owl   *Glaucidium gnoma*

Field marks: 7". Small; **long tail;** no ear tufts; false eyes on back of head; black
streaked flanks. *Voice*–a well-spaced series of mellow *hoo* or *hoo-hoo* whistles.
Status: Rare to uncommon resident in suitable habitat throughout the region and
on VI; unusual resident in NCNP and MRNP; common resident in ONP; rare
resident in CLNP.

The northern pygmy owl inhabits montane forests of the region. More diurnal
than other small owls, it often hunts during the day and takes more birds than other
owls. From its perch on an exposed branch or the top of a tall shrub, the pygmy
owl also takes insects, lizards, and small mammals. Woodpecker holes or similar
cavities provide shelter for 3 or 4 white eggs and, later, its young. The false eyes
on the back of its head may make it look more formidable to potential predators.

Burrowing Owl   *Athene cunicularia*

Field marks: 9". Small; **long, nearly bare legs;** no ear tufts; nests in burrows.
Voice–soft *coo-cooo* or a cackling alarm call.
Status: Local summer resident in dry open areas of the Cascades; absent from the
Coast Mountains; casual on VI; rare winter visitor in ONP; absent from the region's
other national parks.

Most owls nest in trees; burrowing owls, as their name implies, nest in holes in
the ground, usually old prairie dog burrows or burrows confiscated from other
rodents. The owls modify the tunnel and nesting chamber each year by vigorous
digging and scratching. Because of their dependence on abandoned burrows for
nesting, the numbers of burrowing owls have declined along with prairie dog
populations. Burrowing owls are largely diurnal and feed on insects, small reptiles,
and small mammals. When disturbed, they bob and bow before either flying away
a short distance or scurrying into their burrows. When prey is plentiful, they raise
5 to 7 youngsters each year.

Northern Saw-whet Owl   *Aegolius acadicus*

Field marks: 8". Small; **black bill; reddish brown color.** *Voice*–a long series of
single-note whistles.
Status: Rare resident in montane forests throughout the region; rare resident on
VI and in NCNP, MRNP, and CLNP; common breeding resident in ONP.

This small, earless owl takes shelter in old woodpecker holes in a variety of
woodlands, from river bottoms to coniferous forests. It lays 5 or 6 eggs in the
cavity and feeds its young any prey of appropriate size that it can find—usually
insects and mice, but also rats and squirrels. Saw-whets stay at home for most of
the year, but in a harsh winter, they may move to lower elevations in search of
easier hunting. The boreal owl, found at higher elevations in the region, closely
resembles the saw-whet in both appearance and habits. Both owls tolerate
humans, allowing people to approach close to their roosts.

Northern Pygmy-owl   J. L. WASSINK

False eyes of Northern Pygmy-owl
J. L. WASSINK

Burrowing Owl   J. L. WASSINK

Northern Saw-whet Owl   A. G. NELSON

NIGHTJARS (order Caprimulgiformes, family Caprimulgidae) feed in flight by scooping insects out of midair. Short, weak legs barely allow them to waddle around on the ground. They occasionally perch in trees, but perch lengthwise on the branches rather than crosswise like most birds.

Common Nighthawk
Chordeiles minor

Field marks: 8". Mottled brown and gray plumage; tiny beak. *In flight*–long, pointed wings; **white bar on lower wing;** square or slightly notched tail.
Status: Fairly common summer resident in the region; rare migrant and uncommon summer resident on VI and in NCNP and ONP; uncommon summer visitor in MRNP; locally common summer resident in CLNP.

Look for common nighthawks in the early evening, flying about erratically as they pursue insects. Their batlike feeding behavior has resulted in the nickname "bullbat." During the day, nighthawks sometimes perch on fence posts, on low rocks, or on the ground. Common nighthawks feed exclusively on flying insects, which they scoop out of the air with their cavernous mouths. These birds arrive in the Pacific mountains in late May or early June and lay their 2 eggs in late June. They build no nest, instead laying their eggs on the bare ground in an exposed location. In cities, including Portland, nighthawks commonly nest on rooftops, especially those with graveled surfaces.

Common Nighthawk

Common Nighthawk chick

Common Nighthawk chick showing camouflage

SWIFTS AND HUMMINGBIRDS (order Apodiformes).

Apodiformes means "without feet." The members of this order have feet—albeit tiny and weak—but they are masters of flight.

Swifts (family Apodidae) are built for speed, with torpedo-shaped bodies and flat, narrow, swept-back wings. In flight, they resemble swallows, but the swift's wings beat faster. Creatures of the air, they eat, drink, and even breed on the wing.

Vaux's Swift   *Chaetura vauxi*

Field marks: 4½". Uniform brown above; **pale throat and upper breast; slightly rounded tail.**
Status: Fairly common summer resident throughout the region and on VI; common in NCNP; common breeding summer resident in NCNP, ONP, and MRNP; fairly common in CLNP.

The plain brown Vaux's swifts are the most common swifts in the Pacific mountains. They attach their nest to the inside wall of a hollow tree in forested country. Vaux's swifts commonly lay 4 eggs. Both adults help feed the young a diet of regurgitated insects. During fall migration, Vaux's swifts may roost in large flocks, whirling down like a serpentine black rope into a tall, hollow tree or chimney.

Black Swift   *Cypseloides niger*

Field marks: 7". Large; **uniform dark color;** slightly forked tail.
Status: Local summer resident in region, including VI; rare breeder in NCNP and ONP; unusual migrant in MRNP; absent from CLNP.

These inhabitants of steep, narrow canyons place their nests in protected pockets on vertical sidewalls, often near waterfalls. Each pair of black swifts produces a single egg and raises the youngster together, feeding it a diet mostly of flying ants. Superb fliers, black swifts may forage hundreds of miles from the nest in search of insects to sustain their young. During these foraging trips, which may last days at a time, the young survive without food or brooding from the parents.

Vaux's Swift   A. G. NELSON

White bird droppings identify entrance to Black Swift nest (*center*).   J. L. WASSINK

Black Swift on nest   J. L. WASSINK

Hummingbirds (family Trochilidae), the smallest North American birds,

expend the greatest amount of energy per unit of weight of any known animal except insects in flight. To keep up with those energy demands, hummers sip nectar from flowers for calories and eat small insects and spiders for protein. With their long, thin bills and tubelike tongues they reach deep into tubular flowers to obtain nectar. To move efficiently from flower to flower requires remarkable powers of flight, and hummers can do it all: fly forward, fly backward, fly straight up, fly straight down, hover, pivot, and even perform backward somersaults. Among the most brightly colored birds, they wear dazzlingly iridescent colors on their backs, and the males sport distinctive brightly colored iridescent throat patches called gorgets.

Black-chinned Hummingbird — *Archilochus alexandri*

Field marks: 3½". *Male*–**black gorget** with purplish border and a white band. *Female*–green above, white below; small white spot behind eye.
Status: Uncommon summer resident at lower elevations of the Cascades; absent from the Coast Mountains, VI, NCNP, ONP, and MRNP; rare spring migrant in CLNP.

This bird usually inhabits streamsides in dry regions but can also be found in other habitats with abundant flowers. The black-chinned hummingbird captures insects by hawking them from a conspicuous perch like a flycatcher does. In its courtship flight, this hummingbird traces a deep U-shaped figure in the sky. Like most hummers, these build tiny cup-shaped nests of plant parts held together by cobwebs. Black-chinned hummingbirds lay 2 bean-sized eggs that hatch about 20 days later. The mother thrusts her long bill down her youngsters' throats and feeds them by regurgitation. The young fledge in about 3 weeks and are on their own in about 5 weeks.

Rufous Hummingbird — *Selasphorus rufus*

Field marks: 3¾". *Male*–**scarlet gorget; rusty back; orange red sides**. *Female*–green above, white below; **rust patch in center of rump**.
Status: Common summer resident throughout most of the region, VI, NCNP, ONP, MRNP, and in CLNP.

Ranging as far north as Alaska, the rufous are the most northerly of hummingbirds. These aggressive defenders of feeding and nesting territories sometimes attempt to drive away blackbirds and chipmunks as well as other hummingbirds. In normal flight, their wing beats create a subdued hum, and in a rapid dive, they produce a loud whine. Rufous hummingbirds, as well as other hummingbirds, become torpid at night. Torpidity is a state in which the body temperature drops to that of the surrounding air, and both the heart rate and respiration rate decrease dramatically. When nighttime temperatures drop below 60 degrees, the birds may save as much as 98 percent of the energy they would otherwise use to maintain their normal body temperature. In its courtship flight, the male rufous traces an upright oval in the air.

Male Black-chinned Hummingbird   A. G. NELSON

Male Rufous Hummingbird   J. L. WASSINK

Female Rufous Hummingbird at nest   J. L. WASSINK

Calliope Hummingbird
Stellula calliope

Field marks: 3¼". *Male*–**striped scarlet purple gorget;** greenish back; small. *Female*–green back; white underparts; short tail; no rust in center of rump.
Status: Common summer resident west of the Cascade and Coast range crests; rare summer resident in NCNP and CLNP; rare on VI; absent from ONP; uncommon summer resident in MRNP.

The scientific name of this bird loosely means "beautiful little star," referring to its small size and brilliant colors. The smallest bird in North America, the calliope hummingbird is also the second most northerly hummer, behind the rufous. The calliope inhabits the borders of mountain meadows surrounded by coniferous forests as well as alpine areas as high as 11,000 feet. The tiny nest, camouflaged with lichens on the outside, lies under an overhanging branch in a conifer, well hidden and protected from the elements. The calliope's pendulum-like courtship flight traces a shallow U.

KINGFISHERS (order Coraciiformes, family Alcedinidae), as their name
implies, live primarily on fish. These chunky, compact birds have large bills and large heads accentuated by a ragged erectile crest, tiny feet, short tails, and short, rounded wings. They are solitary except while nesting.

Belted Kingfisher
Ceryle alcyon

Field marks: 13". *Male*–**oversized blue head;** white neck; blue back; **large heavy bill; big, unruly crest;** bluish breast band. *Female*–similar but with an **additional chestnut breast band.**
Status: Fairly common resident at the lower elevations of the region, summer resident only at higher elevations; uncommon summer resident in NCNP and CLNP; common summer resident on VI and in ONP; rare summer resident in MRNP.

The belted kingfisher perches on a branch or stump near or over water containing an abundance of small fish. From here it dives headlong into the water in pursuit of fish, amphibians, crustaceans, and aquatic insects. After the speed of the dive carries it completely underwater, the kingfisher emerges, carrying a small hapless creature in its bill. Kingfishers nest in burrows in cut banks, usually along streams but also along roads, borrow pits, or other similar vertical banks. They dig the burrows with their bills, pushing the dirt out with their small feet. The female may lay as many as 8 eggs, which the pair incubates in shifts. Once the youngsters hatch, their voracious appetites keep both adults busy bringing them food.

Male Calliope Hummingbird J. L. WASSINK

Female Calliope Hummingbird J. L. WASSINK

Belted Kingfisher A. MORRIS, VIREO

WOODPECKERS (order Piciformes, family Picidae) have heavy skulls and thick, heavy, chisel-like bills that enable them to reach the wood-boring insects and larvae hidden under tree bark or in rotting wood. Strong feet and claws and stiff tail feathers help them grip vertical surfaces and brace their bodies in position while hammering. Thus equipped, most woodpeckers forage on the trunks and large branches of trees. Some also take insects from the bark, the air, the foliage, and the ground; some eat nuts, berries, and fruit. In spring, woodpeckers drum to attract mates and establish their territories. Most woodpeckers are easily attracted to suet.

Northern Flicker *Colaptes auratus*

Field marks: 12". Gray head and neck with tan forehead; **grayish brown back and belly** with black breast patch and black spots. *In flight*–**red flash** to underside of wings. *Male*–red and black mustache.

Status: Common resident in suitable habitat throughout the region; uncommon resident in NCNP and CLNP; common resident on VI, in ONP, and MRNP.

Flickers reside virtually anywhere there are trees, but they prefer open woodlands to dense forests. Flickers eat berries but feed mostly on ants and other insects they find by probing the ground rather than chipping wood. They excavate new nesting cavities each year in trees, utility poles, and sometimes in the sides of buildings. In these cavities, female flickers lay 6 to 8 eggs. Abandoned flicker holes provide nest sites for other cavity nesters that are unable to excavate their own cavities, including owls, buffleheads, kestrels, and starlings. Flickers drum on a wide variety of structures, including dead snags, power poles, metal chimneys, roof vents, and even the sides of houses, much to the chagrin of the human inhabitant.

Pileated Woodpecker *Dryocopus pileatus*

Field marks: 18". *Male*–**large;** heavy black bill; black-and-white striped head with red mustache and **red forehead and crest;** black body with white wing bars. *Female*–black mustache; red crest.

Status: Rare to uncommon resident throughout the region; uncommon resident on VI, in NCNP, ONP, MRNP, and CLNP.

The dense coniferous forests of the Cascade and Coast ranges are home to the crow-size pileated woodpecker. The pileated seeks out a tall snag or a live aspen in which to hollow out a nesting cavity for its 3 or 4 eggs. A 3½-inch oval entrance hole, usually located between 15 and 70 feet above the ground, is characteristic of pileated woodpeckers. This large, powerful woodpecker can extract insects and larvae that lie too deep in tough wood for other woodpeckers to reach. The pileated flies with strong, irregular wing beats and its drumming is loud and distinctive.

Female Northern Flicker J. L. WASSINK

Male Northern Flicker J. L. WASSINK

Young Pileated Woodpeckers J. L. WASSINK

Pileated Woodpecker L. KAISER

Lewis' Woodpecker
Melanerpes lewis

Field marks: 11". Grayish black back; **rose red breast and belly; dark red face.**
Status: Local summer resident in open forested areas of all but the northern end of the Coast Mountains; very rare on VI; rare resident in NCNP, ONP, and MRNP.

The Lewis' woodpecker's feeding habits are unique among woodpeckers—it catches insects on the wing, sometimes hawking them from the air like a flycatcher does. It also feeds on fruits and nuts when those foods are available. When moving through its habitat of open pine forests, the Lewis' woodpecker often perches on fence posts or stumps rather than clinging to the sides of a tree or other perch like most woodpeckers do. It nests in dead trees and in abandoned cavities drilled by other woodpeckers.

Yellow-bellied Sapsucker
Sphyrapicus varius

Field marks: 8". *Male*–black with white spots above, light below; **patches of red on crown, nape, and throat.** *Female*–lacks red on nape and throat.
Status: Fairly common summer resident throughout most of the region, most common in the east; very rare on VI; rare resident in NCNP and CLNP; rare in ONP; common resident in MRNP.

The form of the yellow-bellied sapsucker found in this region is the red-naped sapsucker. It frequents all types of woodlands but seems to prefer spruce and aspen groves, which provide the bird both food and shelter. Sapsuckers drill a parallel series of ¼-inch-diameter holes in the bark of alders, willows, and many other trees. The holes, drilled at a slightly downward angle, fill with sap. Sapsuckers eat the sap and the insects attracted by the flowing liquid. They also feed extensively on the cambium layer of inner bark. Sapsuckers excavate nest holes in live trees to house their 4 to 6 white eggs and the resulting young. Fed a rich diet of sap and insects, the young grow quickly and leave the nest about a month after hatching.

Red-breasted Sapsucker
Sphyrapicus ruber

Field marks: 8". Black with white spots above, light below; **red hood and upper breast.**
Status: Uncommon but widespread west of the Cascade and Coast range crests; rare resident in NCNP and MRNP; uncommon resident on VI and in ONP and CLNP.

The habits of the red-breasted sapsucker are virtually identical to those of the red-naped sapsucker. Unlike other sapsuckers, the sexes of the red-breasted sapsucker look alike. During the breeding season, these birds respond vocally when intruders come too close to the nest. For the rest of the year, they are quiet and retiring.

Lewis' Woodpecker   T. J. ULRICH

Male Yellow-bellied Sapsucker at sapwells   **Red-breasted Sapsucker**
L. KAISER   B. RANDALL, VIREO

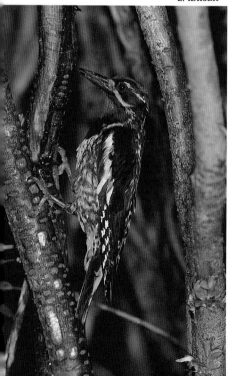

Downy Woodpecker

Picoides pubescens

Field marks: 6". Black-and-white plumage; **white underparts;** white back; black wings barred with white; **bill half the length of the head; outer tail feathers with two or more black bars.** *Male*–red patch on nape.

Status: Common resident throughout most of the region; uncommon resident in NCNP; common resident on VI and in ONP; occasional resident in MRNP; rare summer visitor in CLNP.

The downy woodpecker is one of the most common and widespread woodpeckers in North America. It uses all types of wooded habitat, foraging on the small upper and outer branches and twigs. Watch this bird as it taps on a branch, moves on, taps again, and finally chips away at the wood when it detects a likely insect tunnel. Once it breaches the tunnel, the bird snakes its long, barbed tongue down the hole, entangles the insect or grub, withdraws, and eats it. In summer, the downy takes insects from the surface of branches and foliage. In winter, when food is less plentiful, this woodpecker spends more time chipping for its meals. It regularly visits suet feeders provided by bird-watchers. The downy shares its habitat with the similar, but larger and more powerful, hairy woodpecker. The hairy woodpecker forages more often on the large branches than does the downy.

Hairy Woodpecker

Picoides villosus

Field marks: 8". Black-and-white plumage; white back; black wings barred with white; **bill longer than half the length of head; white outer tail feathers usually unmarked.** *Male*–red patch on nape.

Status: Uncommon to common resident throughout most of the region; uncommon resident on VI and in NCNP and MRNP; common resident in ONP and CLNP.

The hairy woodpecker requires habitat similar to the downy's, but unlike the downy, it does not frequent small woodlots. The hairy woodpecker feeds on the larvae of wood-boring beetles, particularly the western pine bark beetle. This bird feeds more on the trunk and large vertical branches of the trees than the downy does. The hairy woodpecker is also shyer than the downy and usually flies ahead of an intruder rather than moving upward in the tree as the downy tends to do.

Three-toed Woodpecker

Picoides tridactylus

Field marks: 9". **Barred, ladderlike,** black-and-white pattern on back and flanks. *Male*–yellow crown; **three toes** (most woodpeckers have four toes).

Status: Local resident throughout the region; rare resident in NCNP, MRNP, and CLNP; rare on VI and in ONP.

Three-toed woodpeckers claim their territories in newly and severely burned-over forests, moving into the area almost immediately after a fire. They chip off flakes of bark to expose bark-boring beetles that infest the recently killed trees. Three-toed woodpeckers drill cavities in a dead spruce or fir for their nests and raise 4 or 5 young. After 4 or 5 years' use, the birds move on, leaving the nesting holes for bluebirds, nuthatches, and other cavity-nesting birds incapable of drilling their own.

Female Downy Woodpecker
J. L. WASSINK

Male Downy Woodpecker
J. L. WASSINK

Hairy Woodpecker
L. KAISER

Male Three-toed Woodpecker
J. L. WASSINK

PERCHING BIRDS (order Passeriformes) comprise almost three-fifths of

all living birds. Both size extremes, from the 2-foot-long raven to the 4- to 6-inch-long kinglets, live in this region. Some of the most adaptive and intelligent members of the bird world are passerines. The common feature of perching birds is feet with four highly movable toes—three toes pointing forward and one backward—that are ideally suited to gripping a twig, branch, wire, reed, or grass stem. Muscles and tendons automatically tighten their grip if the bird begins to fall backward.

Tyrant Flycatchers (family Tyrannidae) include the flycatchers, pewees,

phoebes, and kingbirds. The family is named for its members' habit of catching flying insects on the wing. The birds sit quietly on a perch from which they dart into the air to snap up insects, often with an audible click of the bill. These tyrants fiercely defend their nesting territories. Most species are neutral shades of gray, brown, olive green, and yellow. Although some species are best distinquished by voice, the presence or absence of an eye ring and wing bars and the color of bill will help you identify the species.

Eastern Kingbird   *Tyrannus tyrannus*

Field marks: 9". Slate gray head and upperparts; concealed red crown patch; **white underparts;** broad fan-shaped tail tipped with broad white band.
Status: Common summer resident east of the Cascade and Coast range crests; rare summer resident in NCNP; rare summer visitor on VI and in ONP; absent from MRNP and CLNP.

As it flies with short, quick wing beats, the eastern kingbird's wings seem to quiver. Conspicuous, noisy, and aggressive, a kingbird will fearlessly attack a hawk, crow, or any other bird that enters its territory. This bird frequents open country with scattered trees, often near water. It waits on an exposed perch, occasionally flying out to snap up an insect. In addition to the more than 200 species of insects it eats, the eastern kingbird dines on the fruits and seeds of more than 40 different plant species.

Western Kingbird   *Tyrannus verticalis*

Field marks: 9". Pale gray head and upperparts; concealed red crown patch; white throat; **pale yellow underparts;** white edges on tail.
Status: Common summer resident east of the Cascade and Coast range crests, rare in the west; rare summer resident in NCNP and ONP; absent from VI, MRNP, and CLNP.

The western kingbird frequents dry open country with scattered trees and shrubs. It darts out from a conspicuous perch in a tree, low bush, fence, or tall weed to catch and eat insects. The western kingbird is less aggressive than its eastern cousin, sometimes even sharing its nesting tree with others of its kind. Western kingbirds usually build their bulky nests in trees but also use bushes, utility poles, water towers, electrical substations, windmills, and many other unexpected locations.

Eastern Kingbird J. L. WASSINK

Western Kingbird R. K. BOWERS, VIREO

Say's Phoebe

Sayornis saya

Field marks: 8". Brown back; **rusty brown on lower breast and belly;** twitches tail downward.

Status: Fairly common summer resident east of the Cascade and Coast range crests; birds scatter during migration; rare summer resident in NCNP; absent from VI andMRNP; rare migrant in ONP and CLNP.

A typical flycatcher, the Say's phoebe snatches its insect meals from the air. It inhabits arid country usually away from water—dry sagebrush, grassland prairies, and sunny canyons. It also lives in agricultural areas, nesting around ranch buildings, in niches in rock walls, and on cut banks—anywhere with a firm shelf to support the nest. Built without mud, the nest is a flat structure of grasses lined with wool and hair.

Willow Flycatcher

Empidonax traillii

Field marks: 6". Brownish green back, whitish underparts; faint eye ring; orange lower mandible. **Song is a dry *FITZ-bew*** while that of the very similar alder flycatcher is *fee-BEE-o.*

Status: Regular summer resident throughout much of the region; unusual summer resident in NCNP; common summer resident on VI and in ONP; rare summer resident in MRNP; absent from CLNP.

The willow flycatcher occupies a wide variety of habitats—from brushy fields and weedlots to willow thickets and open woodlands. This bird catches most insects in flight. The willow flycatcher places its well-hidden nest low in a tree or bush.

Although you will easily recognize the willow flycatcher as a member of the *Empidonax* genus of flycatchers, you will run into difficulty identifying the species. Experts generally agree that *Empidonax* flycatchers display greater differences in plumage between individuals within a species than they do between species. All the *Empidonax* flycatchers look much like the bird in the photograph. Their songs best distinguish them in the field. Identify the willow flycatcher by its *FITZ-bew* call, which emphasizes the first syllable. The call of the alder flycatcher stresses the second syllable.

Western Wood-pewee

Contopus sordidulus

Field marks: 8". Dusky gray brown plumage; **two white wing bars; no eye ring; dull dark bill.** *Voice*–a nasal descending *pheer.*

Status: Uncommon to common summer resident throughout the region; common summer resident in NCNP and MRNP; uncommon on VI and in ONP and CLNP.

The western wood-pewee often perches on a dead branch at the edge of a forest clearing. It periodically flits out to snatch a bee, wasp, ant, fly, or other insect from the air with an audible snap of its bill. This bird beautifully crafts its nest, camouflaging it with lichens, in a crotch of a horizontal branch between 15 and 75 feet above the ground. The female incubates the 3 eggs, which hatch after about 12 days.

Say's Phoebe T. J. ULRICH

Willow Flycatcher J. L. WASSINK

Western Wood-pewee J. L. WASSINK

Larks (family Alaudidae) inhabit short-grass prairies and other areas with low-growing, sparse grasses. When on the ground, larks walk rather than hop as most birds do. They eat insects and seeds and build their cup-shaped nests under tufts of grass. Larks utter flight songs from as high as 800 feet above the ground.

Horned Lark *Eremophila alpestris*

Field marks: 8". Brown above, white below; **black crown, facial stripe and breast band;** slender bill; horns not always visible.
Status: Common summer resident in the short-grass–sagebrush–alpine tundra areas throughout the region; rare summer resident in NCNP; uncommon summer resident in MRNP; common summer resident on VI and in ONP and CLNP.

The horned lark nests in wide expanses of open country—short, sparse grasses and alpine tundra—where it digs or finds a slight hollow to contain 2 to 5 finely speckled off-white eggs. While courting, the male sings its weak song from a perch on the ground and while circling overhead, sometimes as high as 800 feet. The horned lark walks, instead of hopping like many birds, and seldom perches in trees or shrubs. When feeding, this lark walks or runs over the ground in search of weed seeds, waste grain, and insects.

Swallows (family Hirundinidae) are small, fast-flying, streamlined birds that catch and eat insects on the wing. On long, pointed wings, swallows swoop and glide, often skimming the surface of the water, occasionally dipping to pick a bug off the surface or take a sip of water. On short legs and tiny feet they perch on wires and thin branches but seldom walk. Swallows tolerate humans and often nest in buildings or birdhouses. In fall, they gather in great flocks to feed, roost, and migrate.

Barn Swallow *Hirundo rustica*

Field marks: 7". *Male*–**metallic blue black above; red brown forehead and breast; deeply forked tail.** *Female*–similar but with slightly duller colors.
Status: Common summer resident wherever suitable nesting structures are available; abundant summer resident in NCNP and ONP; common summer resident on VI and in MRNP; rare summer visitor in CLNP.

Swift and graceful, barn swallows are one of the most familiar and best-loved birds in North America. They gather at puddles or on muddy shorelines to collect the mud to construct their cup-shaped nests. Formerly limited by a shortage of suitable cliffs on which to build their nests, these birds have ranged more widely with the spread of civilization and the accompanying proliferation of barns and other buildings in which to nest. Look for barn swallows perching on utility lines or swooping back and forth overhead in pursuit of insects. The closest these birds come to singing is a musical twittering that they usually utter in flight. Barn swallows breed from April to June and fly south in September or early October.

Horned Lark   J. L. WASSINK

Male Barn Swallow   J. L. WASSINK

Barn Swallow at nest   J. L. WASSINK

Cliff Swallow   *Hirundo pyrrhonota*

Field marks: 6". Black crown, back, wings and tail; **dark rufous throat, neck, and rump;** pale forehead; **dark, square-tipped tail.**
Status: Abundant summer resident near suitable buildings throughout the region; abundant summer resident on VI and in NCNP and ONP; absent from MRNP and CLNP.

Cliff swallows build their mud nests on the outsides of bridges, barns, hotels, observation towers, and other buildings as well as on cliffs. These birds build gourd-shaped nests, sometimes stacked on top of one another, in colonies containing as many as 100 pairs of swallows. The side entrance holes usually face downward. Cliff swallows can be seen in the Pacific mountains from April through September.

Violet-green Swallow   *Tachycineta thalassina*

Field marks: 5½". **Dark upperparts with a green or purplish sheen,** white below; white patches on side of rump almost meet over the tail; **white on sides of neck extends up on neck and over eyes.**
Status: Common to abundant summer resident throughout the region; abundant summer resident in NCNP and ONP; common summer resident on VI and in MRNP; uncommon summer visitor at CLNP.

Found only in the western United States, violet-green swallows frequent forests and steep-walled canyons. They seek out a suitable tree cavity, line it with straw and feathers, and lay their four to seven eggs. Unlike the other swallows, they have begun to invade cities and build their nests in cracks and crevices in buildings not already occupied by house sparrows. Violet-greens forage at greater heights than the other swallows. They nest in June or July and fly south again in late August to winter along the Pacific coast of Mexico.

Tree Swallow   *Tachycineta bicolor*

Field marks: 6". *Male–***steely blue black** or green above; white below; triangular wings; square tail. *Female–*similar but with slightly duller colors.
Status: Common to abundant summer resident at lower elevations in the region; uncommon summer resident in NCNP and MRNP; common summer resident on VI and in ONP; absent from CLNP.

Tree swallows are the first swallows to arrive in spring and the last to head south in fall. They prefer more open country, often near water, than does their smaller cousin, the violet-green swallow. Like the violet-green, these are cavity nesters. Tree swallows often nest in aspens and compete with mountain bluebirds, common flickers, and house wrens for available cavities. The only swallows to winter regularly in the United States, tree swallows spend the cold season in Florida, along the Gulf of Mexico, and in central and southern California (along the Salton Sea and the Colorado River).

Cliff Swallow   J. L. WASSINK

Violet-green Swallow   J. L. WASSINK

Tree Swallow   J. L. WASSINK

Bank Swallow   *Riparia riparia*

Field marks: 5". Smallest of the North American swallows; **brown back;** white underparts; **brown breast band;** slightly forked tail. Similar species: rough-winged swallow lacks breast band.
Status: Locally common summer resident east of the Cascade and Coast range crests; rare in the west; rare summer resident in NCNP; rare migrant on VI and in ONP; absent from MRNP and CLNP.

Widespread across North America except in the south and extreme north, these compact swallows nest in colonies in the vertical cuts of riverbanks, gravel pits, or roadsides. Using only their thin, weak feet and tiny bills, they dig a 3-foot tunnel into the bank, at a slightly upward angle to prevent flooding, and lay their 4 to 7 eggs. The bank swallow flies with shallow, rapid wing beats.

Northern Rough-winged Swallow   *Stelgidopteryx serripennis*

Field marks: 5½". Brown back, white below; **no brown breast band;** notched tail.
Status: Rare local summer resident throughout the region; uncommon summer resident on VI and in NCNP and ONP; rare summer resident in MRNP; rare summer visitor in CLNP.

Named for a series of small hooks on the outer edge of the outer primary, the rough-winged swallow uses vertical cutbanks like the bank swallow but nests individually or with colonies of bank swallows rather than in pure colonies. This swallow may dig its burrow in loose soil, or it may take over an abandoned kingfisher hole or rodent burrow. Grasses or bits of plants line the nest chamber, which lies at the end of the 9- to 28-inch-long tunnel. The female lays 6 or 7 eggs. The rough-winged swallow snaps up wasps, bees, flying ants, beetles, flies, and dragonflies flying low to the ground. Slightly larger than the similar bank swallow, the rough-winged swallow has a slower and more fluid tempo to its flight.

Purple Martin   *Progne subis*

Field marks: 8". *Male–***purplish black plumage.** *Female–***dull purplish black above,** grayish below. *In flight–*short triangular wings; long forked tail.
Status: Local in downtown Tacoma and Seattle; few nesting colonies elsewhere; uncommon breeders in ONP; absent from VI and the other national parks.

Well known in the eastern United States, purple martins are rare in the Cascades and absent from the Coast Mountains. Colony nesters, they tradition-ally used old woodpecker holes in snags and suitable small pockets in cliffs. Native Americans put up gourds for martins to nest in. Today, martin boxes provide nesting sites for the vast majority of these birds. Martins capture most of their insect food on the wing but also pick ants, wasps, beetles, and other crawling insects from the ground.

Bank Swallow J. L. WASSINK

Northern Rough-winged Swallow T. J. ULRICH

Male Purple Martin T. J. ULRICH

Jays

Jays (family Corvidae) are among the best-known birds. Large (10 to 25 inches) and conspicuous (black, blue, gray, green, or black and white), intelligent and boisterous, these raucous birds thrive in spite of drastic changes in their environment and persecution by humans. Jays are sturdy birds with stout, pointed bills. Opportunistic, they eat almost anything animal or vegetable—fruits, berries, insects, garbage, and carrion. The sexes look similar, and the nests are bulky structures of twigs and branches. Some species migrate, others do not. Most are gregarious.

Steller's Jay
Cyanocitta stelleri

Field marks: 13". Conspicuous crest; **dark blue with sooty black head and neck.**

Status: Fairly common to common resident of the region's coniferous forests; common resident on VI and in NCNP, ONP, and MRNP; uncommon resident in CLNP.

The western equivalent of the eastern blue jay, the Steller's jay is noisy and boisterous. It inhabits the coniferous forests of the Pacific mountain ranges but characteristically lives in yellow pines. The Steller's jay begins nesting in May, and the young hatch in June. It feeds on seeds, berries, insects, and even the eggs and young of other birds. It's call is a raucous *shack-shack-shack.*

Gray Jay
Perisoreus canadensis

Field marks: 12". *Adult*–**gray plumage; short bill;** white forehead; black nape. *Juvenile*–sooty black.

Status: Fairly common resident of the higher elevation forests throughout the region; uncommon resident in NCNP; abundant resident on VI and in ONP and MRNP; common resident in CLNP.

Also called Canada jays, these residents of lodgepole pine and spruce forests are unafraid of humans. They earned their nickname "camp robbers" by such brazen acts as stealing bread from plates and even bacon from the frying pan. Gray jays have loose, fluffy plumage that allows almost silent flight. Early in the year, when the snow is still on the ground and the temperatures are low, they build their bulky nests in hidden spots in pine or spruce trees.

Black-billed Magpie
Pica pica

Field marks: 20". **Large;** looks **black and white** from a distance and in poor light; shines green/blue metallic when close up; **long tail.**

Status: Common to abundant resident east of the Cascade and Coast range crests; rare in the west; rare summer resident in NCNP; vagrant on VI and in ONP and MRNP; rare resident in CLNP.

This inhabitant of open country is common and highly visible in the sagebrush-grassland habitats of the region's lower elevations. The magpie is bold, inquisitive, and always suspicious. Its loud *mahg* call is easy to recognize. The magpie builds its nest, a large dome-shaped mass of sticks with a side entrance, in a thorny shrub or tree. Owls and other birds and mammals often use the nests after the magpies have deserted them. Magpies walk or hop on the ground while feeding.

Steller's Jay   J. L. WASSINK

Gray Jay   J. L. WASSINK

Black-billed Magpie   J. L. WASSINK

Clark's Nutcracker
Nucifraga columbiana

Field marks: 13". Gray plumage; **long, sharply pointed bill; black and white wings;** short tail; **flashy white wing and tail patches visible in flight.**
Status: Common resident in the upper elevations of the region; uncommon resident in NCNP; rare resident on VI and in ONP; common resident in MRNP; abundant resident in CLNP.

Look for Clark's nutcrackers in openings near extensive stands of conifers, often near timberline, where they use their long bills to extract the seeds from treetop cones. They also gather grubs from the bark, insects from the air, and scraps and handouts from picnickers. Nutcrackers, like some other jays, cache food, returning later to retrieve the stored tidbits, even from under 2 feet of snow.

American Crow
Corvus brachyrhynchos

Field marks: 20". **Jet black plumage; stout bill; call is** *caw, caw, caw.*
Status: Fairly common resident throughout the region, particularly east of the Cascade and Coast range crests; common resident in NCNP and ONP; rare resident on VI and in MRNP; rare summer visitor in CLNP.

American crows usually inhabit farming country with a mix of cultivated fields, pastures, scattered woodlots, and fence rows. They feed on displaced grasshoppers and mice in newly mown hayfields, waste grain in harvested grain fields, and choice tidbits in area landfills. Although wary of humans, crows are taking up residence in cities and towns. With their nests secure in the forks of trees high above the ground, they have access to the food sources provided by humans. After the nesting season, they gather in loose flocks and wander through the countryside in search of food. At dusk, crows come from miles around to spend the night in communal roosts. They use these favored roosts for weeks at a time and may reuse them from year to year.

Common Raven
Corvus corax

Field marks: 24". Large heavy bill; **solid black plumage** but bigger and heavier than the crow; longer wings, wedge-shaped tail; **call is** *croa-a-ak.*
Status: Fairly common resident throughout the region; uncommon breeding resident in NCNP; common breeding resident on VI and in ONP, MRNP, and CLNP.

Common ravens prefer the coniferous forests of the mountains to the farmlands of the flats. Ravens share the opportunistic feeding habits of other jays but also act like raptors, consuming rodents, rabbits, insects, worms, nestling birds, bird eggs, moles, and frogs. They are excellent fliers and may soar like hawks as well as perform acrobatic feats and spectacular dives during courtship. Ravens build bulky stick nests on ledges in open terrain and in steep-walled canyons.

Clark's Nutcracker J. L. WASSINK

American Crow J. L. WASSINK

Common Raven J. L. WASSINK

Titmice and Chickadees (family Paridae), sprite little birds, commonly visit bird feeders. Tolerant of humans, they flit to and fro after seeds that they wedge in crevices and hammer open with their bills. In winter, they feed on dormant insects and spider eggs they glean from the twigs and bark of trees and bushes. Although they are cavity nesters, they cannot excavate a hollow unless the wood is well rotted; consequently, they often finish work on holes begun but abandoned by woodpeckers.

Black-capped Chickadee — *Parus atricapillus*

Field marks: 5¼". Small; gray and white plumage; **black cap and bib;** white cheeks; buffy flanks; *chick-a-dee-dee-dee* **call is diagnostic.**
Status: Common resident throughout the region; less common at upper elevations; uncommon breeding resident in NCNP and ONP; rare resident on VI and in MRNP and CLNP.

Black-capped chickadees prefer deciduous forests and woodlots in the valleys, occupying slightly lower elevations than the similar mountain chickadees. In winter, they are easily attracted to feeders by suet and sunflower seeds. Although chickadees accept birdhouses less readily than wrens and bluebirds do, they use them occasionally.

Mountain Chickadee — *Parus gambeli*

Field marks: 6". Small; gray and white plumage; black cap and bib; **white eyebrow;** white cheeks.
Status: Common in the higher elevations of the region, especially east of the Cascade and Coast range crests; uncommon resident in NCNP; very rare winter visitor on VI and in ONP; common resident in MRNP; abundant resident in CLNP.

Although their ranges overlap somewhat, mountain chickadees prefer drier, more open coniferous woods at slightly higher elevations than do the similar black-capped chickadees. Mountain chickadees build their nests in rotting stumps or snags and raise 2 and sometimes 3 broods with as many as 9 youngsters in each brood. Steadily uttering their hoarse *chick-a-dee,* they search twigs, foliage, and bark for caterpillars, plant lice, and insect eggs.

Chestnut-backed Chickadee — *Parus rufescens*

Field marks: 5". Brown cap; white cheeks; black throat; **chestnut back and flanks.**
Status: Local resident in mountains west of the Cascade and Coast range crests, more common at lower elevations; common resident on VI and in NCNP and ONP; absent from MRNP; rare resident in CLNP.

Chestnut-backed chickadees live in dark, humid coniferous forests west of the Cascade and Coast range crests, where they forage high in the trees for insects. However, they readily come down to feed around crumbling logs, in tangled underbrush, and at well-stocked bird feeders. The call, hardly recognizable as a chickadee, is a harsh, nasal *shik-zee-zee.* The chestnut-backed's nesting habits are similar to those of the other chickadees.

Black-capped Chickadee   J. L. WASSINK

Mountain Chickadee   J. L. WASSINK

Chestnut-backed Chickadee   A. WALTHER, VIREO

Bushtits (family Aegithalidae) are active, acrobatic insect eaters with small bills and long, thin tails. These tiny, plump birds travel in flocks except during the breeding season. When disturbed, they depart with a short, weak, jerky flight on short, rounded wings.

Bushtit   *Psaltriparus minimus*

Field marks: 3½". *Male*–short bill; dark eyes; **dull gray above;** lighter below; no wing bars; **long tail.** *Female*–pale yellow eyes.
Status: Rare resident at lower elevations mostly west of the Cascade crest; absent from NCNP and CLNP; rare resident on VI and in ONP; vagrant in MRNP.

The smallest of the perching birds, bushtits inhabit brushy areas: forest edges, thickets, and suburbs. Both sexes build the long pendantlike, gourd-shaped nests woven of mosses, lichens, leaves, grasses, and other plant materials. The female lays 5 to 7 eggs. Social, bushtits travel in flocks except during the breeding season, twittering constantly to keep in contact with each other.

Dippers (family Cinclidae) orient their lives almost completely around the water. Extremely soft, thick plumage and an exceptionally large preen gland allow them to endure cold temperatures and icy water with impunity. Movable flaps that cover their nostrils, nictitating membranes over their eyes, and strong feet and legs to grasp the rocky bottom enable the dipper to forage underwater for aquatic insects and insect larvae. They may also use their wings to hold themselves on the bottom, a habit that has led some observers to report that these birds "fly" underwater.

American Dipper   *Cinclus mexicanus*

Field marks: 8". Small and **plump; slate gray;** short stubby tail; **bobs up and down.**
Status: Locally common resident along the rushing, tumbling, icy cold mountain streams of the region; common resident on VI and in NCNP, ONP, MRNP, and CLNP.

Watch for American dippers, or "water ouzels," along swift, rocky, mountain streams, usually wading in shallow riffles with their heads submerged or bobbing up and down on a midstream rock, preparing to venture once more into the icy water in pursuit of aquatic insects. Even on extremely cold winter days, dippers wade in the shallows, sometimes disappearing under the ice in search of aquatic insects and tiny fish. When traveling upstream or downstream to foraging areas, the dipper flies over the water, seldom taking shortcuts over land. The female constructs the nest near the water—on a rock wall, under a bridge, or even behind a waterfall. A bulky ball of moss with a side entrance, the nest lies where a constant spray keeps the moss damp and alive, forming a living, growing nest. The dipper's pleasantly melodious song can be heard over the roar of the water.

Bushtit   P. LA TOURRET, VIREO

American Dipper   L. KAISER

Young Dippers at nest   T. J. ULRICH

Nuthatches (family Sittidae) live among tree trunks and larger branches. These small birds have short tails, long wings, and long, slightly upturned bills. Nuthatches glean the bark for insects, spiders, and larvae and also eat the nuts and seeds of conifers. An enlarged hind toe enables them to hunt head-down and find insects overlooked by other "head-up" hunters. Nuthatches are monogamous, defend territories year-round, and lay 5 to 9 eggs in cavity nests. Suet and sunflower seeds attract them to bird feeders.

Red-breasted Nuthatch   *Sitta canadensis*

Field marks: 4½". Small; black crown; black eye line; white eyebrow; **rufous underparts.**
Status: Fairly common resident throughout the region; uncommon resident in NCNP; common resident on VI and in ONP, MRNP, and CLNP.

These birds inhabit open stands of lodgepole and Douglas fir at higher elevations. Red-breasted nuthatches excavate nesting cavities in conifers or conifer snags and, for reasons unknown to humans, smear the entrance hole with pitch. The birds typically fly directly into the hole without perching or pausing at the entrance. Once identified, this nuthatch's loud *yank-yank* call is easy to recognize.

Pygmy Nuthatch   *Sitta pygmaea*

Field marks: 4½". Brownish head; **black eye line;** bluish gray back.
Status: Local resident in pine habitats east of the Cascade and Coast range crests; less common in the west; absent from VI, NCNP, and ONP; rare resident in MRNP; rare summer visitor in CLNP.

The smallest of the nuthatches, the pygmy searches clusters of pine needles at the ends of branches for insects and pine seeds. The quiet habits and soft twittering voice of this seemingly unafraid bird make it an inconspicuous resident of yellow pine habitats. Because of its size, the pygmy nuthatch can nest in cavities too small for other species to use.

Red-breasted Nuthatch feeding young—note pitch at entrance hole J. L. WASSINK

Red-breasted Nuthatch J. L. WASSINK   **Pygmy Nuthatch** B. RANDALL, VIREO

White-breasted Nuthatch *Sitta carolinensis*

Field marks: 6". Black crown; **white face and underparts;** blue-gray back.
Status: Uncommon resident in deciduous habitats throughout the region; rare resident in NCNP and MRNP; very rare winter visitor on VI and in ONP; uncommon resident in CLNP.

The largest of the nuthatches, white-breasted nuthatches occupy a wide variety of deciduous habitats. These birds rub insects around the entrance holes to their nests. The white-breasted nuthatch utters a single call, often including a descending *keer.*

Creepers (family Certhiidae) are small birds that probe the bark of trees for insects and insect larvae with their long, slender, decurved bills. Like woodpeckers, creepers brace themselves with their tails when feeding.

Brown Creeper *Certhia americana*

Field marks: 5". Small; brownish above streaked with white; white below; **fine, decurved bill;** sharp claws; **long, pointed tail.**
Status: Fairly common but inconspicuous resident of forested areas of the region; rare resident in NCNP; common resident on VI and in ONP, MRNP, and CLNP.

Brown creepers inhabit coniferous forests, where they feed mostly on insects they glean from the bark. They find food by spiraling up a tree trunk, dropping to the base of the next tree, and beginning the spiral ascent again. Brown creepers wedge their nests under loose slabs of bark.

White-breasted Nuthatch   J. L. WASSINK

Brown Creeper   A. G. NELSON

Wrens (family Troglodytidae) are small, brown, active birds with slender bills. They feed almost exclusively on insects. You can easily recognize these birds by their habit of cocking their tails over their backs and by their loud, pleasing songs. Wrens build their nests in cavities, in crevices, and in reeds. They prefer to remain hidden in thickets but become bold when intruders venture too close to their nest.

House Wren   *Troglodytes aedon*

Field marks: 5". Gray brown above, pale brown below; slender bill; **barred tail; beautiful song.**
Status: Scattered summer resident throughout the Cascades and the southern tip of the Coast Mountains; rare resident on VI and in NCNP and ONP; vagrant in MRNP; rare migrant and summer visitor in CLNP.

House wrens are cavity nesters with a reputation for nesting in strange places: an old tin can, a cow skull, a pump spigot, the pocket of a discarded coat, or a mail box. Found near thickets in open tree stands, near forest edges, in old orchards, and near old trees and run-down buildings, wrens aggressively compete for nesting cavities. They may puncture the eggs of other birds in the process of evicting them. The males attract the females by singing and by filling as many as 12 nesting cavities with sticks. Once the female decides on a mate, she throws the sticks out of the cavity of her choice and does things her way. Very vocal, house wrens sing their beautiful songs throughout the day.

Rock Wren   *Salpinctes obsoletus*

Field marks: 5". Long thin bill; gray brown above; **long tail with buff tips.**
Status: A common summer resident in the drier rocky areas east of the Cascade and Coast range crests; rare resident in NCNP; vagrant on VI and in ONP and MRNP; locally common resident in CLNP.

Although common in suitable habitat, rock wrens are elusive. They inhabit rocky washes, where they probe cracks and crevices for insects and spiders. Rock wrens tuck their nests, built of fine plant materials and lined with fur or feathers, into protective rock crevices. They often place small pebbles at the entrance to the crevice. Intruders into a rock wren's territory face the bird's persistent scolding.

Marsh Wren   *Cistothorus palustris*

Field marks: 5". Brown plumage; **solid rufous crown; white "eyebrows";** long decurved bill; white-streaked back.
Status: Common summer resident in marshy habitats throughout the region; uncommon resident on VI and in ONP; absent from the region's other national parks.

As its name implies, the marsh wren is a conspicuous resident of cattail and bulrush marshes and wet roadside ditches. After building numerous (up to 35 in some cases) domed nests to attract a female, the male perches high on a rush or cattail and launches its sputtery calls and trills. Once won over, the female moves into one of the nests, leaving the rest vacant. Although most marsh wrens fly to Mexico and the southern border states for the winter, some remain in this region.

House Wren   J. L. WASSINK

Rock Wren   T. J. ULRICH

Marsh Wren   J. L. WASSINK

Mockingbirds (family Mimidae) are superb songsters and are highly territorial. They inhabit open, brushy country and often sing from a conspicuous perch. Their neutral colors—grays, slates, or plain browns—provide camouflage while they build their basin-shaped nests and incubate 3 to 6 blue, green, or grayish eggs. The family name, Mimidae, and the common name, mockingbird, come from this bird's amazing ability to mimic the songs of other birds.

Gray Catbird
Dumetella carolinensis

Field marks: 9". Plain slate gray; **black cap; rusty undertail coverts;** sings notes of song only once.
Status: Fairly common mostly east of the Cascade crest and throughout the Coast Mountains; rare summer resident in NCNP; absent from VI, ONP, MRNP, and CLNP.

Quiet and unobtrusive, gray catbirds are seldom seen by anyone not looking for them. Even then, only their soft *mew* call betrays their presence in thick, brushy streamside areas. They utter this call, which gives them their name, when they are disturbed. Catbirds have a varied repertoire of songs they sing any time of day and night. Insects make up roughly half of their diet, but they also eat fruit and berries. They fashion their rough nests low in a tangle of vines, in a dense hedge, or in a mass of garden shrubs. Nests may contain a wide variety of unusual materials, including shoestrings, bandages, white napkins, and plastic bags. The usual clutch consists of 4 greenish blue eggs.

Sage Thrasher
Oreoscoptes montanus

Field marks: 9". Short, straight bill; **gray brown above;** heavily streaked breast; **white-tipped tail.**
Status: Local summer resident in sagebrush habitats east of the Cascade crest; absent from the Coast Mountains except for extreme southern tip; absent from VI and the region's national parks.

Listen for the sage thrasher's loud, long, beautiful song in the dry sagebrush deserts of the region in early summer. The source of the song can often be spotted perched on a tall sage or flying in large circles over the sage flats. The female gathers coarse twigs, plant stems, and other plant materials to fashion her bulky nest in a low bush. When the 4 or 5 boldly spotted, deep blue eggs hatch, the young consume large numbers of grasshoppers, beetles, caterpillars, and other insects the adults find by hunting on the ground like robins do. After the nesting season, sage thrashers consume wild currants, gooseberries, and serviceberries, among others. As winter approaches, these birds move south to spend the cold months in the southern border states from California to Texas.

Gray Catbird   J. L. WASSINK

Gray Catbird   J. L. WASSINK

Sage Thrasher   J. L. WASSINK

Thrushes (family Muscicapidae, subfamily Turdinae) are small to medium-sized songbirds that live on a mixed diet of insects, invertebrates, and plant materials. Nests are cup-shaped structures built in the crotches of trees or in cavities. Singing ability varies—though some can barely twitter, others are marvelous songsters.

American Robin   *Turdus migratorius*

Field marks: 10". Plump profile; black head; yellow bill; dark gray brown back; **dark red orange breast.**
Status: Common to abundant resident throughout the region; abundant resident on VI and in NCNP and ONP; common summer resident in MRNP and CLNP.

Robins frequent virtually all habitats in the region except marshes. These adaptable birds become tame in cities but remain extremely shy in remote habitats. Robins feed on worms, insects, and fruits (cherries, apples, mountain ash, and cotoneaster). They build their sturdy, grass-lined nests in the crotches of trees and lay up to 6 turquoise blue eggs. The young grow quickly. By the time they leave the nest, they closely resemble the adults except for their densely spotted breasts. Immediately after the first brood leaves the nest, the adults build another nest and raise a second, and sometimes a third, brood.

Varied Thrush   *Ixoreus naevius*

Field marks: 10". *Male*–dark head with **orange eye stripe;** black above, orange below; **black breast band.** *Female*–duller colors; gray breast band.
Status: Uncommon to common in suitable habitat throughout the region; uncommon resident in NCNP; common resident on VI and in ONP and MRNP; locally common resident in CLNP.

Similar to robins in appearance and habits, varied thrushes live in the cool, shady, moist coniferous forests of the Cascade and Coast ranges. More easily heard than seen, varied thrushes utter a long, quavering, melancholy whistle followed by a succession of notes that fade away at the end. During the nesting season, they bring insects and invertebrates, including worms and snails, to their 3 or 4 youngsters. Late in the year they search out fruit and may frequent old orchards.

Townsend's Solitaire   *Myadestes townsendi*

Field marks: 9". Slim; **white eye ring;** gray plumage; **pale salmon wing patches;** long white tail; quiet, shy behavior.
Status: Fairly common resident throughout the region; uncommon resident on VI and in NCNP, ONP, MRNP, and CLNP.

Look for Townsend's solitaires perched on the outermost or topmost branches of small trees along the edges of small clearings in open pine and fir or juniper forests. From these perches, they hawk insects like the flycatchers do. Townsend's solitaires build their nests on or near the ground—under an overhang in a cut bank, or sheltered by a log or stone. The eggs are white and heavily blotched. Townsend's solitaires sing their beautiful song—a long series of loud, rapidly warbled, clear notes—from the tops of tall trees or while in flight.

American Robin J. L. WASSINK

Varied Thrush J. L. WASSINK

Townsend's Solitaire J. L. WASSINK

Hermit Thrush
Catharus guttatus

Field marks: 7". Olive brown back; buffy face and eye ring; white below; spotted buff breast; **reddish brown tail.**

Status: Rare to common summer resident throughout the region; uncommon summer resident in NCNP; common summer resident on VI and in ONP, MRNP, and CLNP.

An inhabitant of the high mountains, the hermit thrush prefers the heavy foliage, deep shadows, and damp areas of the region—willow thickets, river woods, and forest undergrowth of mixed conifers and aspen. Sung only during the nesting season, the hermit thrush's serene, flutelike song is one of the most beautiful sounds in nature. The female constructs a large, well-built nest of mosses, plant stems, grasses, and other plant materials 3 to 10 feet up in a bush or conifer. The 4 youngsters are fed primarily insects until they fledge. In fall and winter, fruits and berries become much more important in their diet. Although most hermit thrushes migrate, a few stay in the region, spending their winters in the lowlands. Those that migrate stop in the south border states, making this the only thrush that normally winters in the United States.

Swainson's Thrush
Catharus ustulatus

Field marks: 7". Olive brown back, white below; **buffy face and eye ring;** spotted buff breast.

Status: Common summer resident on VI and throughout the region; common summer resident in NCNP, ONP, and CLNP; uncommon summer resident in MRNP.

These inhabitants of large stands of mixed conifers and deciduous brush and trees live quietly and are easily overlooked. Swainson's thrushes sing their ascending flutelike song at dawn and at dusk. The rest of the day, they feed on the ground, searching through the forest litter for worms, grubs, and invertebrates. They also feed on berries when available. The female builds her nest on a horizontal branch near the trunk of a small tree or bush. The 3 or 4 blue eggs splotched with brown hatch in about 14 days. After the youngsters fledge, they wander for several weeks before beginning the long migration to Central America.

Hermit Thrush

R. CURTIS, VIREO

Swainson's Thrush   J. L. WASSINK   Swainson's Thrush   J. L. WASSINK

Western Bluebird

Sialia mexicana

Field marks: 6". *Male*–deep blue back, throat, and wings; **rusty breast; chestnut patch on upper back;** hunched appearance. *Female*–grayish; rust tint to breast; bluish wings and tail.

Status: Fairly common to uncommon summer resident throughout the region; rare summer resident on VI and in NCNP, ONP, and MRNP; uncommon summer resident in CLNP.

Inhabitants of the middle to low elevations, western bluebirds frequent forest edges, open forests, roadsides, and farmlands. They search out a tree cavity, line it with grasses, and lay 4 or 5 pale blue eggs. Like other bluebirds, the young grow up on insects the adults either hawk from the air or pick off the ground. In fall and winter, berries augment their diet. Following the nesting season, which usually produces 2 broods, western bluebirds gather in flocks and wander in search of food until the next breeding season. Not as migratory as mountain bluebirds, western bluebirds may winter on their breeding range or in nearby lowlands. The main concern for the future of these inhabitants of open timberlands is the loss of nest cavities through logging, replacement of wooden fence posts by metal fence posts, and competition with starlings, wrens, tree swallows, and sparrows. Concerned birders can counteract this problem by providing birdhouses.

Mountain Bluebird

Sialia currucoides

Field marks: 6½". *Male*–**sky blue plumage;** *female*–duller gray with blue tinge on wings.

Status: Common summer resident in the drier habitats of the eastern part of the region, less common in the more humid west; uncommon summer resident in NCNP and MRNP; very rare on VI and in ONP; common summer resident in CLNP.

Mountain bluebirds arrive early to this region, often when snow is still on the ground. They select an open territory near a snag or other suitable nesting cavity in sagebrush grasslands or mountain meadows. Mountain bluebirds snap up insects, their main food, from the ground or out of the air. In fall and winter, berries supplement their diet. Unlike other bluebirds, mountain bluebirds often hover when pursuing insects. After raising the young, usually 2 broods at the lower elevations, the family groups form large flocks before heading south. A few mountain bluebirds may remain in the region throughout the winter. As with the western bluebird, the availability of nesting cavities limits its distribution. In areas with suitable open areas, putting up nest boxes can increase populations dramatically.

Female Western Bluebird   J. L. WASSINK

Male Western Bluebird   J. L. WASSINK

Female Mountain Bluebird   J. L. WASSINK

Male Mountain Bluebird   J. L. WASSINK

Kinglets (family Muscicapidae, subfamily Sylviinae) are tiny, active insect eaters.
Flighty birds, they forage near the ground but nest in the tops of conifers, often in Douglas firs. Kinglets tuck their deep, semipensile nest in the fork of a horizontal branch where it is well hidden in the needles. Kinglets lay 8 or 9 eggs, a large clutch for such small birds.

Ruby-crowned Kinglet   *Regulus calendula*

Field marks: 4¼". Small; olive green above; small, thin bill; **broken white eye ring;** two white wing bars. *Male*–red crown patch that flashes when the bird is excited.

Status: Fairly common summer resident in suitable habitat throughout the region; rare resident on VI and in NCNP and ONP; uncommon migrant in MRNP; uncommon migrant and summer resident in CLNP.

One of the smallest of the songbirds, the ruby-crowned kinglet inhabits coniferous forests where it flits and hops among the twigs and leaves in pursuit of insects. Its song, an ascending *liberty, liberty, liberty,* is very loud for such a small singer and is audible at great distances. The male reveals his red crown patch only when he is excited. The only other North American kinglet, the golden-crowned kinglet, has an orange crown edged with black and frequents primarily spruce-fir forests at higher elevations in the Cascades. With the coming of winter, small groups of 3 or 4 kinglets may wander throughout the lowlands west of the Cascade crest.

Wagtails (family Motacillidae) are a predominantly Old World family of small,
slender birds with long tails, long legs, long toes, and elongated claws. Their plumage is inconspicuous, but the birds' elaborate in-flight courtship displays make them highly visible.

American Pipit   *Anthus rubescens*

Field marks: 6½". **Slender profile;** slender bill; brown back; white, lightly streaked underparts; white outer tail feathers; long hind claw; **wags tail as it walks.**

Status: Locally common summer resident in the alpine tundra habitats of the region; common summer resident on VI and in NCNP, ONP, and MRNP; rare summer resident in CLNP.

The alpine tundra is the summer home of these birds. The male sings his courtship song from high in the air and then floats back to the ground on fluttering wings. The female builds the nest on the ground. Sheltered by overhanging vegetation or nestled beside a rock, the female sits tight while incubating her 5 eggs. When fall comes to the high country, the water pipit moves to the lowlands to winter on bare fields, mudflats, and beaches. The water pipit feeds by walking about, plucking insects and seeds from the ground and vegetation. The family designation, wagtail, comes from this bird's habit of continually wagging and flipping its long tail. The call is a two-syllabled *pipit.*

Ruby-crowned Kinglet   P. LA TOURRET, VIREO

American Pipit   T. J. ULRICH

Waxwings (family Bombycillidae) are gregarious birds that live in flocks most of the year. They perch, feed, and fly in squadrons. Waxwings have prominent crests and soft, silky plumage in drab colors. Their common name refers to the waxy tips on the wing coverts. They have short, stout bills adapted for eating fruit, and sturdy legs and feet that allow them to stretch in all directions to reach their meals without falling. Monogamous, they court by passing berries or other objects back and forth. Their weak songs have no known function in courtship. Waxwings wedge their well-built nests on a high branch and lay 3 to 5 bluish gray eggs. They nest later than most birds and feed their young berries and fruit. In late winter, they occasionally eat fermented fruit and behave as if drunk.

Bohemian Waxwing   *Bombycilla garrulus*

Field marks: 8". Pale gray plumage; black mask; **crest; red waxy tips on wing coverts;** yellow and **white spots in wings;** chestnut undertail coverts.
Status: Irregular winter visitor throughout the region; resident in northern Cascades and the Coast Mountains; rare resident in NCNP; very rare winter visitor on VI and in ONP; absent from MRNP and CLNP.

Larger, grayer, and with a more northern distribution than cedar waxwings, Bohemian waxwings inhabit open conifer and mixed woodlands, where they build their nests in conifers. These birds often pass inedible objects, such as sticks and pebbles, back and forth in courtship displays. In summer, they sometimes hawk insects out of the air like flycatchers do. Nomadic in winter, they travel erratically in search of plentiful supplies of berries, sometimes wandering far south of their normal range.

Cedar Waxwing   *Bombycilla cedrorum*

Field marks: 7". Pale brown plumage; black mask; **brown crest; red waxy tips on wing coverts; yellow-tipped tail.**
Status: Fairly common summer resident and irregular winter visitor throughout the region; uncommon summer resident on VI and in NCNP, ONP, and MRNP; rare summer visitor in CLNP.

An inhabitant of brushlands mixed with second-growth timber, cedar waxwings often hawk insects from a conspicuous perch like flycatchers do. The call is a high-pitched *zee.* The courtship display usually involves exchanging an edible object, such as a berry or petal, and ends when one of the birds eats the object. The female builds the nest from 4 to 50 feet above the ground in a conifer or deciduous bush. Depending on where they locate an abundant supply of berries or fruit, cedar waxwings may winter anywhere from southern Canada to Panama. Squadrons of these birds often descend on cities and eat the berries of ornamental trees.

Bohemian Waxwing   J. L. WASSINK

Cedar Waxwing feeding young   J. L. WASSINK

Cedar Waxwings   J. L. WASSINK

Shrikes (family Laniidae) are songbirds that act like birds of prey. They feed on large insects, small lizards, mice, and small birds, which they kill with their powerful hook-tipped bill. Like the birds of prey, shrikes use their powerful feet to tear prey into bite-sized pieces. If the prey is not consumed immediately, they impale it on a thorn or barbed wire for later.

Loggerhead Shrike   *Lanius ludovicianus*

Field marks: 9". Gray, white, and black plumage; **heavy hooked bill;** big head; **broad black mask that meets over bill;** rapid wing beats; long, thin tail.
Status: Rare summer resident east of the Cascade crest; absent from the Coast Mountains, VI, and the region's national parks.

The loggerhead shrike most often dwells in open country, where you can see it sitting quietly on a telephone wire beside a road or perching on the highest twig of a tree or bush. From that perch it searches the ground for any movement that might betray the presence of a mouse, small birds, or large insect. Once a shrike captures its prey, the bird either immediately eats it, feeds it to its nestlings, or stores it for later consumption by impaling it on a nearby thorn bush or barbed-wire fence. Both sexes assist in building the bulky nest deep in a low bush, which provides a home for 4 to 7 youngsters.

Starlings (family Sturnidae) were brought to New York from Europe by a man who wanted to introduce to North America all the birds mentioned by Shakespeare. Starlings have proliferated and displaced other more colorful and tamer birds, such as bluebirds and swallows, from nesting cavities, earning starlings the disdain of modern birders. Starlings have stout, straight bills and large, strong feet and legs—equipment ideally suited to a bird that feeds on virtually anything it can locate while walking on the ground.

European Starling   *Sturnus vulgaris*

Field marks: 8". Plump; glossy black, iridescent plumage; **long yellow bill; short tail;** walks with a waddle. *Winter*–spotted plumage; dark bill.
Status: Abundant resident or summer resident throughout the region, on VI, and in ONP; uncommon to rare summer resident in NCNP and MRNP; absent from CLNP.

These adaptable European immigrants inhabit cities or short-grass farmlands with nearby nesting cavities. They lay 4 to 6 blue or bluish white eggs. These much-despised birds aggressively compete for nesting cavities, displacing native species of bluebirds and swallows—birds many people prefer to starlings. Far from musical, their seemingly ceaseless calling and squabbling consists of various squeaks, chirps, and whistles. Starlings usually gather from the ground their highly variable diet of insects, cherries, and seeds. In fall and winter, they join huge flocks to feed and roost. The communal roosts quickly become a nuisance to humans living nearby.

Loggerhead Shrike   J. L. WASSINK

European Starling   J. L. WASSINK

Young European Starling   J. L. WASSINK

Vireos (family Vireonidae) are small, plain birds that are difficult to observe but easy to hear. Vireo means "I am green" and suits this family well. Vireos sport a stout bill with a slight hook on the upper mandible. These deliberate birds feed on insects they pluck off the foliage of the understory. The nest, a neat basket decorated with bits of lichen, sits in the fork of a sapling and holds 2 to 5 white eggs. Both sexes help incubate and feed the young. Persistent songsters, the males of some of the species may even sing from the nest while incubating the eggs.

Warbling Vireo
Vireo gilvus

Field marks: 5½". Light gray above, whitish below; **whitish eyebrow; no wing bars.**
Status: Uncommon to common summer resident throughout the region; uncommon summer resident in NCNP and CLNP; common summer resident on VI and in ONP and MRNP.

You will find this inconspicuous bird high in the tops of alder thickets and open deciduous woodlands. The warbling vireo moves deliberately through the trees as it gleans insects from the foliage. The male, singing along the way, accompanies the female as she builds the nest, but he does not help her with the construction. The female lines the well-made nest with fine grasses and then suspends it from a fork in a small tree. The male helps incubate the usually 4, white, lightly spotted eggs, often singing as he does so. The distinctive, husky, warbling song of this vireo often ends on a rising note. Warbling vireos winter in Mexico and Central America.

Red-eyed Vireo
Vireo olivaceus

Field marks: 6". Olive green above, whitish below; **gray crown; white eyebrow with black borders;** dark eye line; red eyes.
Status: Rare to uncommon summer resident; uncommon breeding resident in NCNP; absent from MRNP; rare summer resident on VI and in ONP and CLNP.

Although this is the most common bird of the eastern deciduous forests, it is less abundant here in the Cascade and Coast ranges. The red-eyed vireo frequents streamside deciduous trees and aspen-poplar groves. Its almost continuous singing has earned it the nickname "preacher-bird." One bird sang 22,197 songs in a 10-hour period during a summer day! Both sexes build the nest, but the female incubates the 4 eggs alone. Like the other vireos, the red-eyed gleans insects, mostly caterpillars and moths, as it works its way through the undergrowth. This vireo migrates as far as 3,000 miles to winter in the Amazon basin of South America, where it travels in small flocks from one fruiting tree to another.

Warbling Vireo   J. L. WASSINK

Red-eyed Vireo   J. L. WASSINK

Warblers (family Emberizidae, subfamily Parulinae) are small, typically brightly colored birds that pick insects from leaves and twigs of trees and shrubs with their slender, pointed bills. Some warblers frequent the forest floor, others inhabit reeds, brushy streamsides, or treetops. Intensely territorial, they defend their turf with their thin wiry songs. They build cup-shaped nests in the fork of a branch and lay from 3 to 6 eggs. The males are generally brightly colored, the females duller. Warblers migrate to Mexico and South America in winter. The continuing destruction of their wintering grounds poses a serious threat to the population stability of these birds.

Yellow Warbler   *Dendroica petechia*

Field marks: 5". *Male–***orange yellow plumage;** rusty streaks on breast. *Female–* yellow green plumage.
Status: Common summer resident throughout the region, on VI, and in ONP; uncommon in NCNP and MRNP; rare in CLNP.

Yellow warblers are the best known and most widely distributed of the warblers. They inhabit streamside thickets of willow, alder, and cottonwood. Within those thickets, they hunt caterpillars, cankerworms, measuring worms, moth larvae, bark beetles, weevils, and similar creatures. The female, accompanied by the male, builds the nest in a vertical crotch of a bush or tree, sometimes as high as 60 feet above the ground. Brown-headed cowbirds often parasitize yellow warblers by laying their eggs in with the warbler's. If the warbler discovers the addition, it may construct a new floor over the cowbird egg and begin a new clutch of its own.

Yellow-rumped Warbler   *Dendroica coronata*

Field marks: 5". *Male–*dark gray plumage; **yellow patches on crown, throat, sides and rump;** white wing patches. *Female–*grayish brown plumage.
Status: Common summer resident throughout the region; uncommon summer resident in NCNP and MRNP; abundant summer resident on VI and in ONP and CLNP.

The yellow-rumped warbler dwells among the twigs and branches of medium-sized trees, where it moves almost constantly—darting, flitting, hanging upside down, and hawking insects. It inhabits mixed woods and usually nests in the top of a conifer. On its winter range, this warbler feeds heavily on fruit, mostly bayberry and wax myrtle. This species consists of two varieties that interbreed where their breeding ranges meet. The "Audubon's warbler," distinguishable by its yellow throat, breeds in the Cascade and Coast ranges. The "Myrtle warbler," with a white throat and less white in its wings, nests farther north in central to northern Canada and Alaska but is a regular migrant through this region.

Female Yellow Warbler   J. L. WASSINK

Male Yellow Warbler at nest
J. L. WASSINK

Female Yellow-rumped Warbler
J. L. WASSINK

Male Yellow-rumped Warbler
J. L. WASSINK

Common Yellowthroat   *Geothlypis trichas*

Field marks: 5". Small; *Male*–olive brown above; **black mask; yellow throat.** *Female*–olive brown above; yellow throat.
Status: Common summer resident throughout the region, on VI, and in ONP; uncommon summer resident in NCNP; occasional summer resident in MRNP; absent from CLNP.

Common yellowthroats are common inhabitants of thick, damp shrubbery and brushy undergrowth, usually near open water. Because of the dense habitat and the bird's shy nature, the yellowthroat's song is often the easiest way to detect it. The male regularly sings from within the lush growth while searching for small grasshoppers, beetles, moths, and other insects, but also periodically ascends to the uppermost branches of favored shrubs to proclaim his territory, calling *witchety, witchety, witchety.* Highly territorial, yellowthroats loudly scold trespassers on their turf. The birds build their well-hidden nest near or on the ground. They feed by gleaning insects from the leaves of shrubs, grasses, and weeds. Like many of the other wood warblers, yellowthroats fall victim to a cowbird's egg deposit and may bury the unwanted egg beneath a second floor in the nest before laying another clutch of 4 eggs.

Weaver Finches (family Passeridae) are primarily an Old World family of

birds. Named for the nest-weaving habits of some of its members—who weave the most complex and largest nests in the bird world—weaver finches have short, conical bills adapted to cracking seeds. Two introduced species represent this family in North America: the Eurasian tree sparrow and the house sparrow. Only the house sparrow is found in the Pacific Mountain ranges.

House Sparrow   *Passer domesticus*

Field marks: 6". *Male*–brown and gray plumage; black bill; gray crown; **black throat and upper breast;** white cheeks; **chestnut nape;** white wing bars. *Female*–gray brown plumage; gray below; pale "eyebrow."
Status: Abundant resident around developed areas throughout the region, absent from remote habitats; uncommon resident in NCNP; common resident on VI and in ONP; rare summer resident in MRNP; absent from CLNP.

The house sparrow is another introduced species that has flourished in the United States and Canada. Bold and impudent, yet suspicious and wary, these birds were brought from Great Britain and introduced into Brooklyn, New York, in the 1850s. They have since taken up residence wherever human construction leaves small cracks or crevices that provide access for nesting. Into those openings, house sparrows pack grass, paper, and feathers to form a rather messy nest. Where crevices are not available, they construct round, dome-shaped nests in trees or shrubs. These noisy and gregarious birds feed on seeds and whatever scraps of food they can find. Aggressive when competing for nest sites and food, they displace many native species, raising the ire of birders everywhere.

Male Common Yellowthroat   J. L. WASSINK   **Female House Sparrow**   J. L. WASSINK

Male House Sparrow   J. L. WASSINK

Blackbirds and Orioles (family Emberizidae, subfamily Icterinae) are highly visible, vocal birds. They frequently perch on fence posts or on tall reeds and cattails. Their strong, sharply pointed bills enable them to eat a wide variety of food including insects, seeds, grains, and berries. Many of the species are dimorphic; the males and females look different. These birds typically gather in mixed flocks with other blackbirds and starlings after the breeding season.

Red-winged Blackbird   *Agelaius phoeniceus*

Field marks: 9". *Male*–black plumage; sharply pointed bill; **scarlet wing patch with yellow border.** *Female*–heavily streaked brown plumage; sharply pointed bill; reddish tint on shoulder.
Status: Abundant summer resident in the lower elevations of the region; uncommon summer resident in NCNP; common summer resident on VI and in ONP and MRNP; rare summer resident in CLNP.

Among the first migrant passerines to return to the Pacific Northwest mountains in the spring, the red-winged blackbird's arrival is a sure sign that warmer weather is on its way. The males return to this region as early as February and set up territories in the cattails or along wet borders. Several females may nest in the territory of a single male. The females suspend the loosely woven cups in clumps of last year's cattails and line the nests with fine grasses. Although they traditionally nested only in marshes, red-winged blackbirds are beginning to colonize grassy fields away from water. Corn, grain, fruit, and weed seeds provide nutrition during most of the year except for the breeding season, when the young are raised on insects. After raising the young, the adults stay in the marshes while they molt their tail feathers. Some birds winter in this region, but most fly south. Call is a loud *oak-a-leeee-o.*

Yellow-headed Blackbird   *Xanthocephalus xanthocephalus*

Field marks: 10". *Male*–black body; **yellow head, neck, and chest;** white wing patches visible in flight. *Female*–dark grayish brown plumage; pale yellow throat and chest.
Status: Abundant summer resident east of the Cascade and Coast range crests, rare elsewhere; rare summer resident in NCNP; rare summer visitor on VI and in ONP; absent from MRNP and CLNP.

Yellow-headed blackbirds arrive about a month after their red-winged cousins. As with the red-wings, the males arrive first to set up their territories in localized colonies. They pick a conspicuous perch near water from which to sing and display. Their song is harsh and unmusical, something like the creaking of a rusty gate. When the females arrive, they choose a nest site and mate with the male who "owns" that territory. Where yellow-headed blackbirds and red-winged blackbirds share the same marsh, they tend to nest in distinct colonies. Yellow-headed blackbirds usually occupy the cattails and reeds in deeper water. The red-wings nest in shallower water.

Female Red-winged Blackbird
J. L. WASSINK

Male Red-winged Blackbird
J. L. WASSINK

Female Yellow-headed Blackbird
J. L. WASSINK

Male Yellow-headed Blackbird
J. L. WASSINK

Brewer's Blackbird
Euphagus cyanocephalus

Field marks: 9". *Male*–iridescent black plumage; sharply pointed bill; purplish gloss on head; greenish gloss on body; **whitish eye.** *Female*–grayish brown plumage; sharply pointed bill; dark eye.

Status: Fairly common to common summer resident throughout the region; uncommon resident on VI and in NCNP; common year-round resident in ONP; rare summer visitor in MRNP; rare summer visitor in CLNP.

Once strictly a bird of the western United States and Canada, the Brewer's blackbird is extending its range eastward across the prairies. The dryland version of the red-winged blackbird, the Brewer's blackbird forages on the ground for insects and seeds. As it walks, it jerks its head in a characteristic manner. The Brewer's blackbird builds a mud and grass nest low in a bush or tree or on the ground, lining it with fine plant materials or hair.

Brown-headed Cowbird
Molothrus ater

Field marks: 7". *Male*–black body; **brown head; short conical bill;** stubby tail. *Female*–gray brown plumage; **short conical bill;** stubby tail.

Status: Fairly common summer resident throughout the region; rare winter resident at lower elevations; uncommon summer resident in NCNP; common summer resident on VI and in ONP; vagrant in MRNP; rare summer resident in CLNP.

Brown-headed cowbirds follow grazing cattle or horses to feed on grasshoppers and other insects that the moving animals stir up. Occasionally a cowbird will perch on the back of one of the animals for a free ride. These birds live along woodland edges, in sagebrush, in creek bottoms and brushy thickets, and near agricultural lands. Cowbirds do not build their own nests or raise their own young. Instead, a female will lay single eggs in the nests of as many as 10 or 12 other birds and let the adopted parents care for them. Yellow warblers, song sparrows, red-winged blackbirds, and western wood-pewees are a few of the over 200 species of birds that have served as foster parents to cowbirds. Cowbird eggs hatch in 10 days, usually before those of the host. The young cowbird grows quickly and is usually able to outcompete the rightful nestlings. Although naturally wary, cowbirds can be attracted to ground feeders with mixed birdseed.

Brewer's Blackbird   J. L. WASSINK

Male Brown-headed Cowbird   J. L. WASSINK

Female Brown-headed Cowbird   J. L. WASSINK

Western Meadowlark

Sturnella neglecta

Field marks: 9". Plump profile; streaked brown plumage; long pointed bill; **yellow breast; black neck band; short tail with white outer tail feathers;** tail flicks almost constantly.

Status: Common to abundant summer resident in virtually all sagebrush and grassland habitats within the region, especially east of the Cascade and Coast range crests; rare summer resident on VI and in NCNP, ONP, and CLNP; vagrant in MRNP.

The western meadowlark inhabits open grasslands, cultivated fields, and pastures. These common migrants build their grass nests on the ground in surprisingly short vegetation, camouflaging the nest by weaving an overhanging dome from nearby grasses. They raise their young on a diet of beetles, crickets, grasshoppers, caterpillars, wasps, ants, spiders, and seeds. Watch for meadowlarks perched on posts or wires, singing their beautiful, exuberant, liquid song. As houses replace the open grasslands they require, meadowlarks disappear, creating concern about their future in areas of limited grasslands west of the Cascades.

Northern Oriole

Icterus galbula

Field marks: 8". *Male*–long pointed bill; **black cap, eye line,** throat and back; **orange cheeks, sides, belly, and rump;** black wings with white shoulder patches. *Female*–yellowish gray plumage; dark wings with white wing bars.

Status: fairly common local summer resident throughout the region, although less so west of the Cascade and Coast range crests; rare summer resident on VI and in NCNP and ONP; absent from MRNP and CLNP.

Northern orioles live in the treetops where they search for insects. The semipensile, sac-shaped nest hangs from the tips of the branches of a large tree—typically a cottonwood, oak, or other streamside tree. The song is a loud flutelike warble. Two races of northern orioles occur in the United States and southern Canada: the "Bullock's" oriole, found in this region, is replaced in the east by the "Baltimore" oriole. The "Bullock's" oriole has orange cheeks; the "Baltimore" oriole has black cheeks. These birds come to feeders that offer fruit and sugar water.

Western Meadowlark A. CAREY, VIREO

Male Northern Oriole T. J. ULRICH

Female Northern Oriole J. L. WASSINK

Tanagers (family Emberizidae, subfamily Thraupinae) are predominantly tropical birds—of 242 species, only a couple inhabit the temperate regions. The males have brilliantly colored plumage and both sexes sport stout bills. They are monogamous, and most sing either weak songs or no songs at all. Tanagers eat insects, fruit, and nectar.

Western Tanager   *Piranga ludoviciana*

Field marks: 7". *Male* **black and yellow plumage;** stout bill; **orange red head;** black wings and tail; one yellow and one white wing bar. *Female*–yellow gray plumage; stout bill; gray back; two thin wing bars.

Status: Fairly common summer resident in coniferous habitats throughout the region; uncommon summer resident in NCNP and MRNP; common summer resident on VI and in ONP and CLNP.

These brightly colored summer visitors inhabit open conifers, mixed forests of spruce-fir, lodgepole pine, and Douglas fir-aspen habitats at elevations to 10,000 feet. Quiet feeders, they search the treetops for caterpillars and insects, usually simply gleaning bugs while moving through the upper branches. They also flycatch from high limbs. Tanagers typically place their shallow saucerlike nest in a fork near the end of a branch midway up an evergreen tree. The male does not incubate but does help feed the young. The western tanager's casual song, drifting down from the treetops, is a common sound in the Cascade and Coast ranges and the easiest way to detect the bird's presence. With the approach of winter and the subsequent decline in insect populations, western tanagers migrate to Mexico and Costa Rica. Attract tanagers to feeders with dried fruit, oranges, and cake.

Grosbeaks, Buntings, and Sparrows (family Emberizidae, subfamily Coerebinae) are small, seed-eating birds. Their conical bills are pointed at the tip for picking up seeds and heavy at the base for cracking them. Coloration varies from dull to brilliant. Their songs are generally beautiful.

Black-headed Grosbeak   *Pheucticus melanocephalus*

Field marks: 8". *Male*–stout, light-colored bill; black head; orange neck, breast, belly, and rump; black back and wings with white markings. *Female*–buff and brown instead of black and orange; striped head; finely streaked flanks.

Status: Fairly common summer resident throughout the region; uncommon summer resident in NCNP; common summer resident on VI and in ONP; rare summer resident in MRNP; absent from CLNP.

Male black-headed grosbeaks usually arrive in the southern Cascades about 6 days before the females. They scatter through a broad range of habitats—riparian woodlands, second-growth forests, forest edges, orchards, and suburbs—and sing to claim their territories. When the females arrive, the males sing from nearby branches, then suddenly fly in the air, continuing to sing. The females build loose nests in the outer branches of trees or shrubs near forest openings, and deposit 3 or 4 eggs. Both sexes incubate and feed the young. These birds hunt caterpillars, grasshoppers, bees, wasps, and other insects. Ripe cherries, blackberries, raspberries, and other fruits and berries seasonally supplement their diets. Black-headed grosbeaks winter in Mexico.

Male Western Tanager   J. L. WASSINK

Female Western Tanager   J. L. WASSINK

Black-headed Grosbeak   D. & M. ZIMMERMAN, VIREO

Evening Grosbeak
Coccothraustes vespertinus

Field marks: 8". Big, clumsy-looking birds; olive neck and chest; yellow back and belly; **heavy powerful bill; black wings with large white wing patches.** *Male*–heavy yellow eyebrow. *Female*–duller colors than the male.

Status: Fairly common local resident throughout the region; uncommon resident on VI and in NCNP and ONP; rare resident in MRNP; uncommon in CLNP.

Evening grosbeaks roam the region's coniferous forests. In fall, following the breeding season, they often gather into large flocks and sporadically appear at abundant food supplies, such as areas with abundant cone crops or well-stocked bird feeders. Their bills have adapted to crack hard seeds and extract the nuts from conifer cones. Evening grosbeaks love sunflower seeds, and flocks of them may spend most of the winter at a single feeder. They also love the seeds of box elders, willows, maples, and elms as well as ripening chokecherries.

Lazuli Bunting
Passerina amoena

Field marks: 6". *Male*–**blue head; stubby bill;** blue back and wings; orange brown breast and flanks; **white wing bars;** white belly. *Female*–grayish brown above, buff below; pale wing bars.

Status: Fairly common summer resident throughout the Cascades, particularly east of the crest; absent from the Coast Mountains and VI; accidental in ONP; uncommon summer resident in NCNP; vagrant in MRNP; rare summer resident in CLNP.

Lazuli buntings are birds of shrubbery, thickets, and tangled second-growth timber dotted with grassy openings. They sing from utility wires or exposed branches while nervously flicking their tails. In addition to seeds, they sometimes eat insects they hunt on the ground. Lazuli buntings place their nest, woven of coarse grasses and lined with finer materials and hair, low in the shrubbery. The female incubates the 4 eggs alone, but the male helps feed the young. They winter from southern Arizona to Baja California and central Mexico.

Male Evening Grosbeak J. L. WASSINK

Male Lazuli Bunting J. L. WASSINK

Female Lazuli Bunting J. L. WASSINK

Finches' (family Fringillidae) lives revolve around their food supply. These seed eaters have stout bills with an internal groove to hold the seed in place while the large jaw muscles help crush it. Finches use their tongue to peel and discard the husk. The swallowed kernel passes to the powerful gizzard to be digested. Because finches feed above the snow line, they can, and do, nest in any season, timing their nesting to coincide with an abundant supply of seeds. The female builds the cup-shaped nest and incubates the eggs. Both sexes feed the young. While most other birds rely on insects to provide enough protein to their rapidly growing youngsters, several of the finches (crossbills, siskins, and redpolls) raise their young on a diet exclusively of seeds. The adults gather large quantities of seeds in their gullets and return at infrequent intervals (20 to 60 minutes) to the nest to regurgitate seeds for their youngsters. Finches nest solitarily or in loose colonies and defend only a small area immediately around the nest. They often gather in flocks and forage away from the nest wherever they can find an abundance of seeds. When not breeding, they wander erratically in search of food.

Rosy Finch   *Leucosticte arctoa*

Field marks: 6". **Reddish belly, flanks, and rump;** streaked brown plumage; black forehead; **gray crown.**
Status: Fairly common resident in the alpine tundra of the region; rare resident on VI and in NCNP and ONP; common summer resident in MRNP; uncommon resident in CLNP.

Rosy finches are birds of the mountaintops. They summer on the alpine meadows of the region, often above 7,000 feet in Washington and British Columbia, constructing a cup-shaped nest in a well-concealed crevice or niche in the rocks. They forage on the ground for seeds and insects, often scouring the margins of melting snowbanks for wind-blown food. During the breeding season, they develop cheek pouches for carrying food—a feature that allows them to conserve energy by carrying large amounts of food on each trip. Rosy finches have long, pointed wings to counteract the strong winds at high elevations. With the first severe snowstorm of the season, they gather in flocks and seek out grassy meadows on the high plateaus of the lower elevations, even venturing as low as the foothills in some years. There they roost in rock crevices and feed on the ground on weed and grass seed.

Pine Grosbeak   *Pinicola enucleator*

Field marks: 9". *Male*–**reddish pink plumage; short heavy bill;** white wing bars. *Female*–olive gray plumage; short heavy bill.
Status: Rare to uncommon permanent resident in the coniferous forests of the region, particularly in the Coast Mountains; rare resident in NCNP; uncommon summer resident on VI and in ONP and MRNP; rare summer visitor in CLNP.

The largest of the finches, pine grosbeaks have rounded bills ideally suited to their diet of needle buds and berries. They are also capable of extracting and crushing pine seeds. These plump, slow-moving birds of the subalpine coniferous forests build their nests in the low branches of subalpine firs or Engelmann spruce. As winter approaches, pine grosbeaks move to lower elevations to feed on piñon nuts or the fruit of ornamental trees. Their song is a musical warbling.

Rosy Finch (gray-crowned)   J. L. WASSINK

Male Pine Grosbeak   J. L. WASSINK

Female Pine Grosbeak   J. L. WASSINK

Purple Finch
Carpodacus purpureus

Field marks: 5½". *Male*–wine red head, throat and breast; reddish wash on back and breast; notched tail. *Female*–**whitish "eyebrow"** and lower cheek; mottled brown above, heavily streaked below; notched tail. *Voice*–distinctive sharp metallic *tick* uttered in flight.

Status: Common resident in lower elevations of the region, particularly west of the Cascade and Coast range crests; less common at higher elevations; rare resident in NCNP; common resident on VI and in ONP; vagrant in MRNP; rare summer visitor in CLNP.

Purple finches inhabit mixed forests, open woodlands, and suburbs. Primarily seed eaters, they also eat apple, birch and aspen buds, insects, and caterpillars, and various fruits as they ripen. In the Cascade and Coast ranges, purple finches nest 5 to 60 feet up in Douglas firs, building neat cups of plant materials lined with mosses, fine grasses, and hair. The female lays 4 greenish blue spotted eggs and incubates them herself. The male may bring food to the incubating female.

Cassin's Finch
Carpodacus cassinii

Field marks: 6". *Male*–heavily streaked plumage; **reddish wash on head and throat; light unstreaked belly.** *Female*–heavily streaked plumage. *Voice*–distinctive double or triple note call in flight.

Status: Fairly common residents at higher elevations and east of the Cascade and Coast range crests; rare resident in NCNP; accidental in ONP; uncommon summer resident in MRNP; common resident in CLNP.

Cassin's finches make their homes in coniferous forests at higher elevations than purple finches do. They seek open, dry forests or forest edges. During the spring breeding season, male Cassin's finches sing a varied, liquid, warbling song. Their nesting habits are similar to those of the purple finch.

House Finch
Carpodacus mexicanus

Field marks: 5". *Male*–**short, stout bill;** streaked brown plumage; red forehead, eyebrow, and throat; **streaked sides.** *Female*–heavily streaked brown plumage.

Status: Abundant in cities and near farms throughout the Cascades, rare at upper elevations; distribution in the Coast Mountains limited to the southern portion east of the crest; rare resident in NCNP; common resident on VI and in ONP; absent from MRNP; rare summer visitor in CLNP.

House finches prefer the lowlands of the region and commonly inhabit open woodlands and urban areas. They have adapted well to humans and have begun nesting in the abundant nooks and crannies of buildings. Unlike most songbirds, they do not carry out the fecal sacs of the young, and the nests get rather messy. Like the other finches, house finches feed primarily on seeds but also eat buds, flowers, and insects. They have a loud melodious song. Males in some areas have a yellow wash on the forehead and breast instead of the usual red wash, possibly the result of differences in diet. House finches visit feeders with millet or sunflower seeds.

Male Purple Finch   T. J. ULRICH

Male House Finch   J. L. WASSINK

Cassin's Finch pair   J. L. WASSINK

Red Crossbill
Loxia curvirostra

Field marks: 6". *Male*–brick red plumage; **crossed mandibles; black unbarred wings.** *Female*–olive gray plumage; **crossed mandibles;** unbarred wings.
Status: Irregular local resident in the region; rare resident in NCNP; uncommon resident on VI and in ONP; uncommon summer resident in MRNP; common resident in CLNP.

Red crossbills live in coniferous forests with abundant cone crops. The birds dangle upside down to extract seeds and snip off cones. They carry the cones to perches and hold them down with one foot while they extract the seeds. The crossed tips of their bills allow them to pry open the tough pine, spruce, and fir cones while their tongues scoop out the seeds. The red crossbill's bold and deliberate manner allows birders to closely observe.

Red crossbills are unique in that they nest almost any time of year when sufficient conifer seeds are available—even when the days are short and snow blankets the ground. Where pine seeds are available, red crossbills nest in the spring. In larch forests, they nest in late summer. Where they depend on spruce seeds, crossbills nest in fall and early winter. In mixed spruce and pine forests, nesting may extend over 10 months of the year. When not breeding, they wander erratically, searching for abundant supplies of cones.

White-winged Crossbill
Loxia leucoptera

Field marks: 6½". *Male*–bright pink plumage; black wings with **white wing bars; crossed mandibles.** *Female*–olive gray plumage; dark wings with **white wing bars; crossed mandibles.**
Status: Irregular in the region, more common in the Coast Mountains than in the Cascades; rare resident in NCNP; rare winter visitor on VI and in ONP; rare summer visitor in MRNP; absent from CLNP.

White-winged crossbills nest in northern boreal forests from just south of the Canadian border north to central Alaska. Except for favored nesting localities, these crossbills are found in the region only in winter. Even then they normally wander only as far south as Washington, but their erratic wanderings may occasionally take them farther south along the ranges.

Although they feed mostly on seeds and nest when this food is available, white-winged crossbills also eat insects. They are attracted to big-game salt licks and salted highways, where they lick up the salt with their tongue. They will frequent bird feeders stocked with sunflower seeds.

Like the red crossbill, the female white-winged crossbill builds her deeply cupped nest in a thick tuft of needles well out on a conifer branch from 5 to 80 feet above the ground. Mosses, fine grasses, and fur line the loosely constructed arrangement of twigs, rootlets, and bark strips, which holds the 4, pale blue, heavily blotched eggs. Although he does not help incubate, the male brings the female food while she sits on the eggs.

Male Red Crossbill   J. L. WASSINK

Female Red Crossbill   J. L. WASSINK

Male White-winged Crossbill   J. L. WASSINK

Common Redpoll
Carduelis flammea

Field marks: 5". Brown and gray streaked plumage; **red cap; black chin;** pink breast; heavily streaked flanks.

Status: Local visitor throughout the region; irregular migrant in NCNP; rare winter visitor on VI and in ONP; vagrant in MRNP; rare summer visitor in CLNP

Common redpolls breed in the subarctic forests of northern Canada. In winter, they sometimes move south into this region and wander erratically in search of suitable food supplies—weed patches, birch cones, and well-supplied bird feeders. They prefer the open habitats of desert shrub, sagebrush, grasslands, and urban areas.

Pine Siskin
Carduelis pinus

Field marks: 5". Small; thin, pointed bill; **heavily streaked brown above,** streaked white below; **yellow often visible in wings and at base of tail.**

Status: Common resident in the coniferous forests of the region, on VI, and in NCNP, ONP, MRNP, and CLNP.

Noisy, gregarious, and nomadic, pine siskins fly in groups year-round, uttering light twittering notes that seem to be synchronized with their wing beats. These treetop birds often hang upside down as they use their tweezerlike bills to extract the seeds of small cones or while feeding on tree buds and small leaves. They also eat dandelion seeds when available. Pine siskins raise their broods in well-constructed, compact nests of dry roots, grasses, and leaves set well up in a conifer. Their tame dispositions make them a joy at feeders, where they come readily to thistle (niger) seeds. Their call is a rising, high-pitched, buzzy trill. Like many finches, pine siskins wander erratically in winter.

American Goldfinch
Carduelis tristis

Field marks: 5". *Male*–**bright black and yellow plumage;** black forehead; yellow body; **black wings** with white wing bars; black tail. *Female*–greenish yellow color; **black wings** with white wing bars; black tail.

Status: Fairly common seasonal resident in lower elevations of the region; rare resident in NCNP; common summer resident on VI and in ONP; rare summer resident in MRNP; absent from CLNP.

The American goldfinch, Washington's state bird, depends on thistles. They line their nests with thistle down, nest when thistle seeds mature, and raise their young on a diet of thistle seeds. Consequently, they are the last birds in the region to start nesting. Their tweezerlike bills are ideal for extracting seeds from thistles and other composites. The American goldfinch is the only bird capable of eating teasel seeds, which are located at the base of long, spiked tubes. After the nesting season, goldfinches gather in flocks to forage in open weedy fields and thickets. Their call is *per-chic-er-re*. Attract them to feeders stocked with thistle seeds.

Common Redpoll   T. J. ULRICH

Pine Siskin   J. L. WASSINK   **Male American Goldfinch**   J. L. WASSINK

Towhees and Sparrows (family Emberizidae, subfamily Emberizinae)

are small birds (4 to 7 inches) with predominantly dull gray or brown plumage. You can identify these birds primarily on the basis of subtle but distinctive plumage characteristics, including face, crown, and breast patterns. One or more sparrows occupy all habitats in the region.

Green-tailed Towhee   *Pipilo chlorurus*

Field marks: 7". Slender; **rufous cap;** gray green above; **white throat;** greenish tail.
Status: Fairly common summer resident east of the Cascade crest from southern Washington south; absent from the Coast Mountains, VI, ONP, and MRNP; vagrant in NCNP; uncommon summer resident in CLNP.

Listen for these secretive birds as they sing from exposed perches in brushy transitional habitats. Their song consists of a series of clear notes followed by a coarse trill or a peculiar catlike *mew.* When they are not singing, the sparrowlike birds feed on the ground beneath low bushes on open mountainsides or high sagebrush plains. They scratch for insects and seeds by simultaneously kicking back with both feet. When disturbed, green-tailed towhees fly just above the ground while pumping their tails. Attract them to feeders with bread, birdseed, or grain.

Rufous-sided Towhee   *Pipilo erythrophthalmus*

Field marks: 8". **Black hood and back;** white spots on wings; **rufous sides and flanks;** white breast and belly; flashing white tail patches.
Status: Common summer resident in all but the drier areas of the Cascades and VI; absent from the Coast Mountains and ONP; uncommon summer resident in NCNP; vagrant in MRNP; rare fall migrant in CLNP.

The western variant of this widely distributed species was once called the spotted towhee because of the numerous white spots on its back. Open woods with brushy undergrowth provide cover for the rufous-sided towhee as it feeds among dead leaves, scratching the ground with both feet at once. Shy, yet one of the most common backyard birds in the Cascades, the rufous-sided towhee regularly visits bird feeders in search of seeds. Its rather unmusical song says its name, *tow-eee.* This towhee locates its bulky nest on the ground or low in a dense bush, never more than 5 feet above the ground. Fashioned in 4 or 5 days by the female, the nest is built from plant materials and lined with fine grasses and other bits of soft plant material. The 3 or 4 grayish eggs hatch in about 12 days, fledge in another 10 days, and fly 2 days after that. Rufous-sided towhees commonly raise 2 broods each season. Following the nesting season, the family groups wander down to the western lowlands of this region or move slightly south for the winter.

Green-tailed Towhee   J. L. WASSINK

Rufous-sided Towhee   L. KAISER

American Tree Sparrow
Spizella arborea

Field marks: 6". **Chestnut crown;** dark upper mandible; yellow lower mandible; white wing bars; **grayish breast with central dark spot.**

Status: Fairly common migrant and winter resident throughout lower elevations of the region, particularly east of the Cascade and Coast range crests; rare winter visitor on VI and in ONP; absent from the region's other national parks.

After spending the summer breeding in the arctic scrub of northern Canada and Alaska, where they establish large territories of up to two and a half acres, American tree sparrows move south into the lower Cascades to pass the winter. Few sparrows spend less time in trees than tree sparrows, in spite of their name. Watch for these birds perching on shrubs or small trees in open country or foraging in small bands along brushy roadsides, weedy edges, and marshes.

Chipping Sparrow
Spizella passerina

Field marks: 5½". **Solid rufous crown; "white eyebrow";** black eye line; unstreaked gray below.

Status: Common summer resident throughout the region; uncommon summer resident on VI and in NCNP, ONP, and MRNP; common summer resident in CLNP.

Chipping sparrows are small birds that prefer open areas in dry environments with thinly scattered trees. They tolerate human activity. Their name comes from their song—a series of rapid chips they usually deliver from the outermost branches of a tree. Their nests are hair-lined cups on conifer branches. Chipping sparrows feed on seeds and insects they find on or near the ground.

Lark Sparrow
Chondestes grammacus

Field marks: 6". Streaked brown above; **bold rufous, white, and black head pattern;** black central tail feathers; white corners and outer tail feathers.

Status: Fairly common summer resident in grassland habitats east of the Cascade crest; absent from the Coast Mountains, VI, NCNP, and MRNP; accidental in ONP; rare summer visitor in CLNP.

Look for this boldly colored sparrow in dry, open meadows. During migration, they gather in large flocks in weedy fields and along roadsides where they search for insects and seeds. One of our finest singers, the lark sparrow's song is a series of long, liquid trills and phrases. The lark sparrow conceals its nest in dense vegetation on the ground.

American Tree Sparrow   J. L. WASSINK

Chipping Sparrow   J. L. WASSINK

Lark Sparrow   J. L. WASSINK

Savannah Sparrow
Passerculus sandwichensis

Field marks: 6". Brown streaked plumage; **narrow, yellow eyebrow; notched tail.**

Status: Fairly common summer resident throughout the region, on VI, and in ONP; rare summer resident in NCNP, MRNP, and CLNP.

Throughout the spring, the savannah sparrow sings its weak, lispy song near moist, grassy sites all the way up to timberline. In spite of inhabiting open country, these small, nondescript birds are secretive and hard to identify. When disturbed, they take to the air in a short erratic flight but soon drop back to the ground and vanish by running through the grass. Savannah sparrows build their nests in grass-lined hollows in short grass or sparse vegetation, such as the grassy fringe of a marsh. Depending on the season, they eat insects or seeds. In winter, they move far enough south to avoid the snow.

Fox Sparrow
Passerella iliaca

Field marks: 7". **Large;** grayish brown plumage; **heavily blotched breast;** large dark spot in middle of breast; **rufous tinge in tail.**

Status: Uncommon summer resident throughout the region; rare summer resident in NCNP; common year-round resident on VI and in ONP; uncommon summer resident in MRNP; uncommon summer visitor in CLNP.

The largest sparrow, the fox sparrow forages among the dead leaves of underbrush by kicking back with both feet at once. Stunted conifers at timberline, shrubby avalanche slopes, and dense thickets in the subalpine regions provide the heavy cover this bird loves. In winter, the fox sparrow frequents the brushy undergrowth of valleys.

Song Sparrow
Melospiza melodia

Field marks: 6½". Heavily streaked brown plumage; **large central breast spot.**

Status: Common resident throughout the region, on VI, and in ONP; uncommon summer resident in NCNP and MRNP; rare summer resident in CLNP.

One of the first birds of spring, song sparrows arrive before the snow melts. Tolerant of humans, these birds prefer the cover of shrubbery, hedgerows, brushlands, and forest edges, where they feed on the ground, scratching with both feet at once. When flitting from one bush to another, they often dip their tail. Their cheerful and persistent singing and rich and varied repertoire of songs put song sparrows in the running for the top singer of the bird world. Almost 50 years ago, song sparrows were the subject of a behavioral study by Margaret Nice, a pioneering ornithologist. She traced their life history from territorial establishment and defense by the male to pair bonding, courtship, breeding behavior, nesting, and feeding behavior.

Savannah Sparrow

Fox Sparrow

Song Sparrow

White-crowned Sparrow   *Zonotrichia leucophrys*

Field marks: 6½". Grayish back streaked with black and brown; **black-and-white-striped crown;** gray face, neck, and breast; **pink bill;** long tail.
Status: Fairly common summer resident throughout the region, on VI, and in ONP; common winter resident at lower elevations; uncommon summer resident in NCNP and CLNP; vagrant in MRNP.

White-crowned sparrows inhabit dense thickets of shrubs interspersed with open feeding areas, including willow thickets in mountain meadows and along the margins of lakes. The nest is a grass-lined cup on the ground or in the fork of a low willow or conifer. When disturbed, these sparrows utter a metallic *pink*. Attract them to bird feeders with mixed seeds.

Dark-eyed Junco   *Junco hyemalis*

Field marks: 6". Sparrow sized; light pink bill; **dark eyes; gray or black head;** white belly; **white outer tail feathers flash when in flight.** *Slate-colored race*–uniform dark gray above and on breast; white belly. *Oregon race*–black hood; brown back; pinkish sides.
Status: Abundant resident throughout the region; common resident on VI and in NCNP and ONP; abundant resident in MRNP and CLNP.

The name dark-eyed junco includes several different-colored races once considered separate species. The Oregon junco is the most common race in this region. It breeds throughout the Cascade and Coast ranges and into Alaska and is a year-round resident here.

The slate-colored race, although more widespread and common across North America than the Oregon race, breeds mostly in Canada and is present in this region only in winter and while migrating.

Highly adaptable birds, dark-eyed juncos inhabit open forests and clearings in dense forests. They frequent open conifer and aspen-conifer stands with grassy undergrowth. They feed by hopping around on the ground picking up seeds and insects off the surface, instead of scratching like many of the sparrows do.

The females build simple nests of grass on the ground or under trees, rocks, or fallen logs. They lay 3 to 6 blue gray eggs, incubate them, and feed the young without help from the males. They commonly raise 2 broods in a single season. Intruders into the nesting territories face agitated adults who flit nearby, uttering a constant barrage of alarm calls.

Gregarious, dark-eyed juncos usually flock except during the breeding season. As winter approaches, large flocks of these birds move to the lowlands where you can attract them to feeders stocked with millet or other small seeds.

White-crowned Sparrow

Dark-eyed Junco (Oregon)

Slate-colored Junco

Lapland Longspur
Calcarius lapponicus

Field marks: 6". *Male*–**black face and throat; chestnut hind neck separated from black face by white stripe;** mottled brown above, white below. *Female*–duller than male; mottled black on face and breast; buff eyebrow; tan ear patch with black border; light chestnut nape.
Status: Irregular winter visitor in the Coast Mountains and northern Cascades, even more irregular in the south; vagrant in NCNP; rare winter visitor on VI and in ONP; absent from MRNP and CLNP.

Although it is the most numerous and widespread longspur in North America, the lapland longspur is uncommon in this region. It breeds on the tundra of arctic Alaska and Canada and, with the coming of winter, moves south into the United States. Because, in their search for weed seeds, lapland longspurs seek out open fields, short grass, or bare ground, they are more common on the southern Great Plains. Wintering or migrating longspurs often mix with snow buntings and horned larks. Named for their long hind claw, longspurs are difficult to see as they walk about on the ground. When approached too closely, they depart with a peculiar undulating flight.

Snow Bunting
Plectrophenax nivalis

Field marks: 7". *Summer*–white head and belly; black back. *Winter*–mottled buff, white, and black plumage; white belly. *In flight*–**large white wing patches.**
Status: Rare winter migrant in the Coast Mountains and the northern Cascade Range of Washington; rare winter visitor on VI and in ONP and MRNP; absent from NCNP and CLNP.

One of the most northern nesters, snow buntings spend their summers in northern Canada. After raising their young, they remain in the north until snow covers the weed seeds on which they survive, forcing the birds south. Among the most cold tolerant of the small birds, snow buntings gather in large flocks and move only far enough south to find open, snow-free prairies and fields suitable for feeding. Look for them along windswept roadsides in open country.

Male Lapland Longspur   T. J. ULRICH

Female Lapland Longspur   T. J. ULRICH

Snow Bunting   T. J. ULRICH

Glossary

Alpine. Inhabiting or growing in the mountains above timberline.

Altricial. Young that hatch blind, naked, and helpless.

Brackish. Mixture of fresh and salt water.

Brood. Young birds that hatch from a single clutch of eggs.

Cambium. The layer of soft, growing tissue between the bark and wood of trees and shrubs.

Carrion. Dead and decaying flesh.

Clutch. A group of eggs laid by one bird.

Comb. A thick, fleshy growth on the top of the head or above the eye.

Coniferous. Cone-bearing plants.

Crest. A tuft of elongated feathers that extends backward on top of the head.

Crown. The top of the head.

Deciduous. Refers to plants that drop their leaves every year.

Dimorphic. Usually refers to species in which the sexes differ in color but may refer to species that have two different color phases.

Diurnal. Active during the daylight hours.

Emergents. Aquatic plants that are rooted underwater but grow up out of the water, such as reeds and cattails.

Estuary. The mouth of a river where the fresh water meets the sea and where tides influence water levels.

Fledge. The act of leaving the nest; usually occurs after the young are fully feathered and able to fly.

Foliage. Leaves of a tree or bush.

Gizzard. A heavily muscled organ that aids digestion of hard seeds by mechanically grinding them.

Gorget. Brilliant feathers covering the throats of male hummingbirds.

Gregarious. Birds that habitually associate with others in flocks.

Gular. Of, relating to, or situated on the throat.

Hawking. Pursuing or attacking prey while flying.

Horns. Tufts of feathers that extend upward from the sides of the head.

Incubate. To keep eggs warm until they hatch.

Iridescent. Shiny, almost metallic feather color that results from the diffraction of light rays and not from pigmentation; includes the gorgets of male hummingbirds.

Larvae. Immature young of insects and invertebrates.

Lek. A traditional site where male birds of certain species, such as sharp-tailed grouse, gather to perform courtship displays to attract females.

Monogamous. A species that breeds with only one individual during a breeding cycle.

Montane. Pertaining to, growing in, or inhabiting mountainous regions; the lower vegetation belt on the mountains.

Molt. The process of shedding and replacing feathers; molting usually occurs after the breeding season and before the fall migration.

Mustache. A strip of colored feathers that extends backward from the base of the bill.

Nape. The back of the head just above the neck.

Nictitating membrane. A clear secondary eyelid that cleans the eye and protects it during swift flight, underwater swimming, when flying through thick brush, etc.

Nocturnal. Active during the night.

Nomadic. Wandering from place to place, seemingly without a pattern.

Omnivorous. An organism that eats both vegetable and animal matter.

Plumage. The feathers of a bird.

Polygamous. A species that breeds with more than one mate during a single breeding cycle.

Precocious. Well developed; covered with down and able to leave the nest and run about soon after hatching.

Prehensile. Capable of precise movement and adapted for grasping or holding by wrapping around.

Primaries. The outermost and longest flight feathers of the wing.

Prolific. Able to produce large numbers of offspring.

Raptor. A bird of prey, such as a hawk or eagle.

Rump. The back portion of a bird just above the base of the tail feathers.

Scapulars. The group of feathers on the shoulder of the bird, alongside the back.

Scavenger. A bird that feeds on carrion, garbage, or the leftovers of other birds' kills.

Solitary. A bird that prefers to live alone and avoids the company of others of its species.

Spatulate. Spoon shaped.

Species. A group of animals or plants that exhibit common characteristics and that interbreed and produce fertile young when given the opportunity.

Stoop. A swift dive in pursuit of prey, characteristic of many raptors.

Territory. A section of habitat that an individual or breeding pair actively defends against others of its own species.

Thermals. Rising currents of air that result from the unequal heating of the earth's surface; soaring birds commonly ride thermals to gain altitude or remain aloft with minimal effort.

Torpor. A state in which the metabolism drops to abnormally low levels; a means of conserving energy.

Wing coverts. Small feathers that overlap and cover the bases of the large flight feathers.

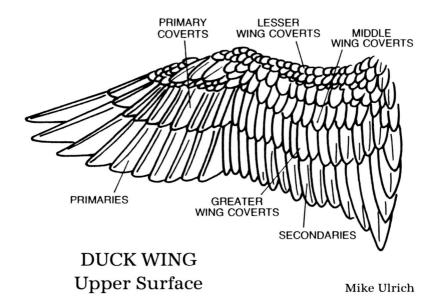

PRIMARY COVERTS

LESSER WING COVERTS

MIDDLE WING COVERTS

PRIMARIES

GREATER WING COVERTS

SECONDARIES

DUCK WING
Upper Surface

Mike Ulrich

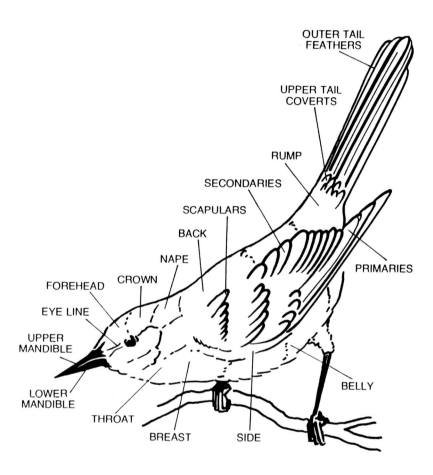

OUTER TAIL
FEATHERS

UPPER TAIL
COVERTS

RUMP

SECONDARIES

SCAPULARS

BACK

NAPE

CROWN

FOREHEAD

EYE LINE

UPPER
MANDIBLE

LOWER
MANDIBLE

THROAT

BREAST

SIDE

BELLY

PRIMARIES

PARTS OF A BIRD

Mike Ulrich

Suggested References

Bird Identification

Campbell, R. Wayne et al. 1990. *The Birds of British Columbia*. Vols. I and II. Victoria, B.C.: The Royal British Columbia Museum.

Farrand, John Jr. 1983. *The Audubon Society Master Guide to Birding*. 3 vols. New York: Alfred A. Knopf.

Harrison, Hal H. 1979. *A Field Guide to Western Birds' Nests*. Boston: Houghton Mifflin.

Kaufman, Kenn. 1990. *Advanced Birding*. Boston: Houghton Mifflin.

Robbins, Chandler S., Bertel Bruun, and Herbert S. Zim. 1983. *Birds of North America*. Racine, Wis.: Golden Press.

Udvardy, Miklos D. F. 1977. *The Audubon Society Field Guide to North American Birds—Western Region*. New York: Alfred A. Knopf.

Bird Behavior

Dennis, John V. 1981. *Beyond the Bird Feeder*. New York: Alfred A. Knopf.

Stokes, Donald W., and Lillian Q. Stokes. 1983. *A Guide to Bird Behavior*. 3 vols. Boston: Little, Brown and Company.

Locating and Observing Birds

Brainerd, John W. 1986. *The Nature Observer's Handbook*. Chester, Conn.: The Globe Pequot Press.

Clark, Jeanne L. 1992. *California Wildlife Viewing Guide*. Helena, Mont.: Falcon Press.

Goodnight, Julie, and Sara Vickerman. 1988. *Oregon Wildlife Viewing Guide*. Lake Oswego, Oreg.: Defenders of Wildlife.

Hanenkrat, Frank T. 1977. *Wildlife Watcher's Handbook*. New York: Winchester Press.

Heintzelman, Donald S. 1979. *A Manual for Bird Watching in the Americas*. New York: Universe Books.

Jones, John Oliver. 1990. *Where the Birds Are*. New York: William Morrow and Company, Inc.

Kress, Stephen W. 1981. *The Audubon Society Handbook for Birders*. New York: Charles Scribner's Sons.

La Tourrette, Joe. 1992. *Washington Wildlife Viewing Guide*. Helena, Mont.: Falcon Press.

McElroy, Thomas P. 1974. *The Habitat Guide to Birding*. New York: Alfred A. Knopf.

Pettingill, Olin Sewall. 1981. *A Guide to Bird Finding West of the Mississippi*. New York: Oxford University Press, New York.

Riley, Laura, and William Riley. 1979. *Guide to the National Wildlife Refuges*. Garden City, N.Y.: Anchor Press/Doubleday.

Wareham, Bill. 1991. *British Columbia Wildlife Viewing Guide*. Edmonton, Alta.: Lone Pine Publishing.

Attracting Birds

Kress, Stephen W. 1985. *The Audubon Society Guide to Attracting Birds*. New York: Charles Scribner's Sons.

Mahnken, Jan. 1983. *Feeding the Birds*. Pownal, Vt.: Garden Way Publishing.

Mahnken, Jan. 1989. *Hosting the Birds*. Pownal, Vt.: Garden Way Publishing.

Bird Songs

Borror, Donald J. 1977. *Songs of Western Birds*. New York: Dover Publications. 12" 33⅓ rpm, record album.

Cornell University Laboratory of Ornithology. 1975. *A Field Guide to Western Bird Songs*. New York: Cornell University. 3 C-60 cassettes.

National Audubon Society. 1977. *Audible Audubon*.

Periodicals and Organizations

American Birds. Published 6 times a year by the National Audubon Society. Contact *American Birds*, 950 Third Avenue, New York, N.Y. 10022.

BC Naturalist. Pubished 6 times a year by the Federation of British Columbia Naturalists. Contact Membership Secretary, Federation of B.C. Naturalists, 3321 - West Broadway, Vancouver, B.C. V6H 4A9.

Birder's World. Published 6 times a year. Contact Birder's World, Inc., 720 E. 8th Street, Holland, Mich. 49423.

Birding. Published 6 times a year by the American Birding Association, Inc. Contact American Birding Association, Inc., Box 4335, Austin, Tex. 78765.

Bird Watcher's Digest. Published 6 times a year. Contact *Bird Watcher's Digest*, P.O. Box 110, Marietta, Ohio 45750.

Cordillera. Published twice year by the Federation of British Columbia Naturalists. Contact *Cordillera*, Subscription Department, Box 473, Vernon, B.C. V1T 6M4.

The Living Bird Quarterly. Published 4 times a year by the Cornell University Laboratory of Ornithology. Contact Cornell University Laboratory of Ornithology, 159 Sapsucker Woods Road, Ithaca, N.Y. 14850.

WildBird. Published monthly. Contact *WildBird* Magazine, P.O. Box 483, Mt. Morris, Ill. 61054-0483.

Index

About the Author

Jan Wassink studied wildlife management at Colorado State University and Utah State University and has photographed wildlife for over twenty years. He wrote and photographed *Birds of the Central Rockies* and *Mammals of the Central Rockies*, published by Mountain Press, and *Idaho Wildlife*, in the American Geographic series. His credits include articles and photographs in *National Wildlife*, *Natural History*, *Ranger Rick*, *Living Bird Quarterly*, *Fur, Fish & Game*, *BBC Wildlife*, *Utah Outdoors*, and *Montana Magazine*.

Wassink lives in Kalispell, Montana, with his wife and three sons.

We encourage you to patronize your local bookstore. Most stores will order any title they do not stock. You may also order directly from Mountain Press, using the order form provided below or by calling our toll-free, 24-hour number and using your VISA, MasterCard, Discover or American Express.

Some other Natural History titles of interest:

____A Field Guide to Nearby Nature	$15.00
____Birds of the Northern Rockies	$12.00
____Birds of the Pacific Northwest Mountains	$14.00
____Botany in a Day	$22.50
____Coastal Wildflowers of the Pacific Northwest	$14.00
____Culinary Herbs for Short-Season Gardners	$20.00
____Desert Wildflowers of North America	$24.00
____Edible and Medicinal Plants of the West	$21.00
____From Earth to Herbalist An Earth-Conscious Guide to Medicinal Plants	$21.00
____An Introduction to Northern California Birds	$14.00
____An Introduction to Southern California Birds	$14.00
____Introduction to Southern California Butterflies	$22.00
____Mountain Plants of the Pacific Northwest	$25.00
____Northern Flights Tracking the Birds and Birders of Michigan's Upper Peninsula	$12.00
____Northwest Weeds The Ugly and Beautiful Villains of Fields, Gardens, and Roadsides	$14.00
____Organic Gardening in Cold Climates	$12.00
____OWLS Whoo are they?	$12.00
____Plants of the Lewis & Clark Expedition	$20.00
____Plants of Waterton-Glacier National Parks and the Northern Rockies	$14.00
____Raptors of the Rockies	$16.00
____Roadside Plants of Southern California	$15.00
____Sagebrush Country A Wildflower Sanctuary	$14.00
____Sierra Nevada Wildflowers	$16.00
____Watchable Birds of the Great Basin	$16.00
____Watchable Birds of the Southwest	$14.00
____Wild Berries of the West	$16.00
____Wyoming Wildflowers	$19.00

Please include $3.00 per order to cover shipping and handling.

Send the books marked above. I enclose $_____

Name_____

Address_____

City_____State_____Zip_____

☐ Payment enclosed (check or money order in U.S. funds)

Bill my: ☐ VISA   ☐ MasterCard   ☐ Discover   ☐ American Express

Card No._____Exp. Date:_____

Signature _____

MOUNTAIN PRESS PUBLISHING COMPANY

P.O. Box 2399 • Missoula, MT 59806
Order Toll Free 1-800-234-5308 • Have your credit card ready.
e-mail: info@mtnpress.com • website: www.mountain-press.com